Turned By Grace

Jeffrey G. Mitchell, Sr.

Jeffrey G. Mitchell, Sr.

TURNED BY GRACE

Jeffrey G. Mitchell, Sr.

Redemption's Story Publishing, LLC, Houston, Texas

Turned By Grace

Turned By Grace

Copyright © 2019
Jeffrey G. Mitchell, Sr.

All Rights Reserved.
No portion of this publication may be reproduced, stored in any electronic system, or transmitted in any form or by any means (electronic, mechanical, photocopy, recording, or otherwise) without written permission from the publisher. Brief quotations may be used in literary reviews.

Print ISBN 13: 978-1-947445-63-5

Some names and identifying details have been changed to protect the privacy of individuals.

Scripture references are taken from the King James Version of the Holy Bible and used with permission from Zondervan via Biblegateway.com.
Public Domain.

For information and bulk ordering, contact:
Pearly Gates Publishing, LLC
Angela Edwards, CEO
P.O. Box 62287
Houston, TX 77205
BestSeller@PearlyGatesPublishing.com

Jeffrey G. Mitchell, Sr.

DEDICATION

Honoring my parents,
James and Sheila Mitchell,
who never gave up on me, even when I was addicted to heroin and at the lowest point in life.
They saw their son; not the addict. I am grateful for the true love of my parents who knew me.

I also dedicate this book to my Godmother,
Joyce Ann Walls,
my brothers and sisters,
James Craig,
Kimberly Mitchell,
Leigh Mitchell,
Craig Mitchell,
and
Kyle Mitchell,
and my children,
Adrienne Mitchell,
Jeffrey Mitchell, Jr.,
Isiah Mitchell,
Brianna Mitchell,
and
Justin Mitchell.

ACKNOWLEDGEMENTS

I wish to thank all who have been a part of my journey—from my past experiences with heroin to finding out you can have a relationship with God.

To my Godmother, **Joyce Ann Walls**, who took me under her wings when I was a small child and even while in my addiction: I thank and love you for continuing to keep me under your wings.

To my **Brothers and Sisters**: We share the same parents and walked similar paths in life, but I had to take this journey alone. I will never forget the memories of our childhood. Love is in my heart for each of you.

To my Cousin, **Troy Mitchell**: I thank you for your devotion and the time you spent with me as I shared my feelings and thoughts about my life. Rest in peace, cousin.

To my Friends, **Sherrodd Bouie, Jeffrey Reaves, Phil Twine,** and **Kim Tyler**: I am grateful for the time we spent growing up together. Now, as men, we still keep in contact. You also gave me some life lessons that helped me become the man I am today. You are my friends for life. Thank you, fellas!

To my Special Friend, **Carmen**: Thanks for everything!

To **Bishop Donald Hilliard, Jr.**: I thank you for opening the doors of the Timothy House. I came to learn that the men and women who served under you were extensions of your love for God. I was able to reconnect with God through the Bible teachings of your leadership. Thank you for the many life-saving sermons. For example, one sermon in particular that you preached at a Men's Only Night on Friday, September 21, 1990, was titled "Dry Bones." In 2002, I just so happened to come across a cassette tape of the same title while I was a resident at The Timothy House. I came to believe God sent me to where my help would come from. *(P.S. I still have that cassette under lock and key because it reminds me of from where God brought me).*

A special thanks to **Pastor David Trawick** for your guidance through your Bible teachings.

To the **Men in The Timothy House**: I am very grateful for each of you. A very special thanks to **Minister Theodore Brown** and **Darrell Roberson** for the life lessons you taught.

To **Pastor Kevin Smallwood**: I am truly grateful for the years I spent with you working at your "Two Fish and Five Loaves" restaurant. I appreciate the love you showed me while I was in The Timothy House.

To **Minister Gary Barnes**: I would like to thank you for "Powerhouses," a Men's Outreach Ministry, which helped me to stay connected to God and for providing a place where I could go on Saturdays to share with other men our struggles in life.

INTRODUCTION

My "Turned By Grace" journey begins in the back seat of a car while waiting for my parents to come out of the house. I sat there and began thinking about the choices I've made in life — especially the ones that got me into the situation I faced.

No future.

No hope.

My self-respect was nonexistent.

Jobless.

Definitely impoverished.

What did I have to show after being on this Earth for 40 years? Where did I go wrong? To whom was I listening?

The date was March 4, 2002. I remember it all so well. That day, I was to be dropped off at a transitional house for men in Perth Amboy, New Jersey. I dreaded the ride there because I had to explain to my mother how I spent all of the money I had on the card but left her the food stamps. Needless to say, she wasn't at all happy about that.

I had been such a disappointment to her as a son, so I really didn't see any reason to change!

I placed myself in this situation, from using heroin for over ten years. I've been in countless recovery settings, detoxes, and in-patient and out-patient programs. The results were always the same: *jail, institutions, and spiritual death.*

Where was my rainbow?

Even as I sat and waited for my parents to get into the car, I used two bags of heroin out of a bundle I had purchased the night before…all because I did not want to go through any withdrawals.

And so, my story begins…

SUNSHINE — A POEM

I awoke to You in the dark of day, for Your hour has not yet come—but the presence of You is known. Your glory is shown on the just and unjust, making a difference in life. You reign up high as well as down low. There is no place that can escape Your light, to the highest mountains and through the lowest valleys. A piercing ray of light breaks through the darkness of night saying, *"Reign sun! Reign over all that I have shown you! I brought you forth to rule over darkness!"* The bright morning star shines so all can see, standing in His rays of light for the comfort and warmth He brings. Who can look upon You without being affected by You? Who can stand before You without knowing Your true worth in the Heavens as well as the Earth?

Jeffrey G. Mitchell, Sr.

TABLE OF CONTENTS

Dedication vi

Acknowledgements vii

Introduction ix

Sunshine — A Poem xi

Chapter One

The Trip to My Transition.. 1

Chapter Two

The Choice: Years or Tears... 5

Chapter Three

My Addiction, My Comforter 10

Chapter Four

Confusion Sets In... 14

Chapter Five

Dope Sick and Saved 16

Chapter Six

I Wanted What He Had 21

Chapter Seven

The Prophet Speaks 24

Chapter Eight

Stop Playing with God!.. 27

Chapter Nine

Baptism Day 30

Chapter Ten

The Enemy's Persistent Pursuit.. 32

Chapter Eleven

Understanding was Just Out of My Reach 36

Turned By Grace

Chapter Twelve
Carried by An Angel 39

Chapter Thirteen
70% Was My New Normal 43

Chapter Fourteen
One-on-One Time with Addiction's Voice 46

Chapter Fifteen
Jeff "The Complainer" 50

Chapter Sixteen
The Enemy is Always Close 53

Chapter Seventeen
Please Don't Leave Me, Lord 56

Chapter Eighteen
Temptation's Knock 60

Chapter Nineteen
The Addictive Spirit Knew Me 62

Chapter Twenty
Focused and Free 64

Chapter Twenty-One
Fond Memories 68

Chapter Twenty-Two
86 Days Clean 70

Chapter Twenty-Three
It Feels Good to Give 75

Chapter Twenty-Four
God Said, "Stop Doing That!" 78

Chapter Twenty-Five
The Healing Rush of Wind 84

Chapter Twenty-Six	
Vicious and the Pup	89
Chapter Twenty-Seven	
Trusting and Believing	96
Chapter Twenty-Eight	
He Was Always There for Me	98
Chapter Twenty-Nine	
It's Not My Birthday!	100
Chapter Thirty	
It's My Birthday!	104
Chapter Thirty-One	
An Unfamiliar Shift in the Atmosphere	106
Chapter Thirty-Two	
The Bee and the Spider	111
Chapter Thirty-Three	
Smarter and Better	112
Chapter Thirty-Four	
197 Days Clean! But Who's Counting?	114
Chapter Thirty-Five	
I Understood Jonah	117
Chapter Thirty-Six	
One Word: Blessed	120
Chapter Thirty-Seven	
Home, Sweet Home	123
Chapter Thirty-Eight	
Familiar Territory	126
Chapter Thirty-Nine	
The Gift of Tongues	129

Turned By Grace

Chapter Forty
The Names of God 132

Chapter Forty-One
"I AM"—A Poem 134

Chapter Forty-Two
The Scattered, Lost Sheep 136

Chapter Forty-Three
The New Student 138

Chapter Forty-Four
Suddenly, I Changed 142

Chapter Forty-Five
Predatorial Instincts 147

Chapter Forty-Six
Lustful Spirits 150

Chapter Forty-Seven
Sin's Trip to Dallas 153

Chapter Forty-Eight
Destiny's Hidden History 158

Chapter Forty-Nine
11 Scriptures for Focusing and Cleansing 162

Chapter Fifty
Proficiency Is Key 164

Chapter Fifty-One
God's Inspiration in Poem 166

Chapter Fifty-Two
"My Beautiful Daughters" – A Poem 168

Chapter Fifty-Three
Strength in Deliverance 170

Chapter Fifty-Four

The Newness of Life 173

Chapter Fifty-Five

My Confession 175

Conclusion 178

Evolving – A Poem 180

About the Author 182

CHAPTER ONE
THE TRIP TO MY TRANSITION

Two weeks prior to joining my parents in the car, I was in a rehabilitation program in Newark, New Jersey at Saint Michael's Hospital. The stay lasted no more than two weeks because I was kicked out for testing positive for using heroin while there. I was caught with just enough drugs in my possession to be considered a "Person of Addiction" (chemically-dependent) and not a drug dealer. I was in desperate need of finding some type of program where I could finally get clean.

~~~~~~~~~~

I see my father exiting the house, making his way to the car. I have to sit up straight so that he doesn't think [know] I'm "on that dope" *(that's how my dad explained people getting high)*. At that moment, though, I was really **FEELING** that heroin.

When he finally got in the car, I asked, *"Where is mom?"* – with a slur to my speech. I was hoping he didn't notice me scratching aimlessly at various parts of my body (also known as the *"addict's itch"*).

"She's in the kitchen," he replied. *"She's on her way out."*

In the back of my mind, I wondered when my mom was going to ask me for the money. As we started down the driveway, my mom turned to me and smiled. I managed to smile back at her. My father asked about the directions to the facility, and my mom told him we needed to take 287 South. She then turned her attention back to me and asked, *"Do you have everything?"*

"Yes," I said as my one word slurred.

"*Are you okay?*" she asked.

"Yeah, mom." It's not as if I wanted to talk about **ANYTHING** at this point this early in the ride.

A few moments pass and my mom asks, *"Do you have the card for me?"* I hesitated one second too long to reply. "**JEFFREY!**" I could hear the irritation in her voice.

"*I spent the money on the card, mom.*"

She sighed and glanced over at my dad. "**ALL** *of it?*" she continued to pry. I didn't want to respond to that question either.

"*I left some food stamps on it.*" I then reached into my pocket, grabbed the card, and handed it to her.

The remainder of the ride to the transitional house was eerily quiet. When we pulled up to the front of the house, I started second-guessing my decision, but I also knew that three years in jail is what the courts offered me as the alternative. I had to either do this now or wait for a new court date and deal with the consequence of not finding a program. I chose to say my goodbyes, so I kissed my mom, told her I loved her, and asked my dad to open the trunk so that I could grab my clothes. As I crossed the street, I turned and waved to my parents as they pulled off, prepared to embark on this new journey.

I approached the door and knocked. From the inside, I heard, *"Come in!"* I pushed open the door and walked into the house. My first stop was at the door on the right, where I placed my bags down just inside the office. I then introduced myself to the person sitting behind the desk. The man replied, *"Hello. My name is Dave. I'm glad you arrived early. I'm expecting two more guys today."* He then instructed me to leave my bags in the office so that he could check my belongings later. I picked them up and put them in the far corner of the office. Dave asked me to have a seat and then began going over some of the house rules, all while I signed papers agreeing to the rules of the program.

As we were talking, I noticed he was not the same person I interviewed with the week prior to get into this place. While Dave talked, I barely heard him. My mind was wandering all over the place. Will he search me? Will he find the drugs I hid on my person? After he finished checking me in and searching through my bags, he told me to head upstairs where the bedrooms were. *"The first room you see when you get to the top of the steps will be where you can put your stuff."*

When I exited the office, I breathed a sigh of relief. Still, I wondered why Dave didn't search *me*. I then heard voices coming from the kitchen area where some of the residents were seated. I assumed it was a group session going on, so I continued on my way. Just as I made it halfway up the steps, Dave yelled from the office, *"Put your stuff away and come back down for group."*

I found my "room" — which was actually in the hallway. It was tight space with a set of bunk beds and two wall units used for closet space. I began placing my belongings on the bottom bunk and then went on the search for a bathroom, which was just off of the second-story kitchen. When I entered the bathroom, I closed and locked the door. I then took out my hidden stash of heroin and snorted half a bag.

I quickly returned to my new living quarters, started to put my things away, and began to make my bed when Dave called out to me from downstairs. *"Come down **NOW!**"* I wiped around my nose and made a quick pitstop in the bathroom to look at myself in the mirror. Not feeling 100% comfortable with my 'look,' I turned on the water, dampened two of my fingers, and sniffed the water so that I could catch that drip.

CHAPTER TWO
THE CHOICE: YEARS OR TEARS

When I finally walked into the kitchen, I took a quick glance around the room before taking a seat at the table. It appeared as if they were waiting on someone to come before starting the group session. I looked around the room again and saw a couple of young men who appeared to be around 20 years old; the others appeared to be around my age and older. As we waited, the other guys began talking about working at the church. We then heard someone coming through the door. Was it the person we were waiting on?

The man who entered the kitchen was the one I met the week prior. He wore a minister's collar this time, unlike the first time we met. *"Good morning, gentlemen,"* he said. Some of the men replied, *"Morning, Minister Boyd."* He then looked directly at me and said, *"Hello. I'm glad you made it."* I smiled and said, *"Thank you."*

Minister Boyd mentioned that we might want to take notes, so I opened my notebook and grabbed my pen. He started by saying, *"Together, we're going to help one another here. We will use the buddy system when we go places. I think God put all of you here so that you can learn and help one another through this program."* He then began the day's discussion: You are not supposed to have sex until you're married. I'm thinking, *"He has to be kidding, right? **NO SEX?!**"*

*Okay. This seems like a good time to stop and explain to **you** how I even ended up at this transitional house…*

Just before Christmas 2001, I was at a house getting high. I was alone at the kitchen table when a voice spoke to me as if in stereo:

"I AM GOING TO LOCK YOU UP!"

I pushed away from the table, stood up, and looked around the room. There was no one else in the kitchen with me, and the voice I heard was not in my head. The words, *"I am going to lock you up,"* passed **THROUGH** my body. I was so nervous, I gathered up the remainder of my drugs and told my friend, ***"I gotta go!"***

I stepped outside onto the porch and immediately took notice of an unmarked police car to my left. I turned to go back inside the house to avoid getting arrested, but I heard them coming after me. I ran full-speed into the bathroom to try and flush down the toilet the drugs I had on me, but they were hot on my heels.

So, there I sat in *"group,"* which was far better than doing a three-year bid in the correctional system. I noticed the minister looking at me, so I decided to sit up straight and give him my full attention.

While my mind wandered, Minister Boyd had changed the topic. He was now talking about lust, self-gratification of the flesh, and how they can control and manipulate what we do. *"Unless you become intimate with God, the lust of the flesh will always be with you,"* he explained. He then asked, *"Is anyone here married or has been married?"* No one spoke up, so I guess that question didn't apply to anyone there.

Just as the group was ending, the doorbell rang. A man had come to get a few of the guys to help clean the church. The minister instructed me to go with them. While going out the door, I passed another man coming into the house with bags in hand. I greeted him with a *"Hello!"* as the rest of us made our way out the door to the church, which was right next door to where we were staying.

The church looked to me as if it used to be a movie theater. They had converted it into a beautiful sanctuary to worship and praise God. The man who came and got us told me to vacuum the rug and said to be sure I went in between the rows of seats and the entrance area as well. I immediately got to task. As I was vacuuming, I found some loose change and placed it into my pocket. By the time I was halfway up the aisle, I had grown tired and was hungry. As I thought about it, I had arrived at 7:30 a.m. and hadn't eaten a thing since before leaving my parents' house that morning. I was ready to take a **BREAK**! Plus, I was asked to clean the glass on the doors, too. I complained silently to myself, *"He's not going to get all of this work done by me! I need help! Heck, I'm not even getting paid for all of this!"*

Jeffrey G. Mitchell, Sr.

After a while, one of the other guys passed by me and said, *"I'm going to the house to start lunch. In half an hour, come on over and eat."* It was if he read my mind! *"Okay,"* I replied.

By the time I finished vacuuming, it was lunchtime. I approached the man who came and got us and said, *"I'm going back to the house to eat."* As I made my way out of the church, I was in awe by the picture of Jesus that was on the wall.

When I entered the house, Minister Boyd asked, *"Is everything okay?"*

"Yeah. I was told to come back here for lunch."

On my way to the kitchen upstairs, I saw the new guy putting his stuff away in our "room." I kept walking. Hot dogs and French fries were on the menu, so I had a seat at the table, feeling completely famished and ready to **EAT**! As I was talking to the man who made the food, I used a few words that included profanity. He looked over at me and said, *"You can't use swear words here."* I then uttered a few more, which prompted another person to explain that I was now part of a **Christian** program and should not be using profanity.

After I finished my food, I went to my room and pushed the stuff I had on my bed to the side so that I could lie down. The new guy spoke and introduced himself as "James." We shook hands as I introduced myself to him. As I laid there, I looked around and noticed three other bedrooms. I do believe the house can hold up to ten men at a time in the program. I thought, *"I'm kind of glad I came early, or I would be the one climbing up that ladder to the top bunk!"* James and I started conversing, but then someone came by and said, *"You're not allowed to lie on your beds now."*

Okay. **NOW** they are starting to bother me with all of this "what I can't do" stuff!

CHAPTER THREE
MY ADDICTION, MY COMFORTER

I decided to look through the handbook I was given when I first got there. I needed to avoid telling the next person who wanted to tell me what I can and can't do how I **REALLY** felt. I found myself walking towards the bathroom—book in hand—to finish off the rest of the heroin I still had hidden on me. I was trying to save it for later, but I was getting upset and frustrated with their rules…and it was just the first day!

I locked the bathroom door and turned on the water so they couldn't hear what I was doing. Plus, I needed some energy before going back to cleaning the church. Almost immediately after I pulled out my stash, there was a knock at the door. *"Someone is in here!"* I yelled.

"I was told to tell you it was time to go back to the church," came the reply from the other side.

"Okay. I'll be there when I'm done in here."

When I was done my dirty deed, I returned to my "room" and noticed James was nowhere around. I made my way downstairs and saw Minister Boyd sitting in the office. He gave me a friendly glance as I continued to walk out the door.

Back at the church, I caught up with James. He and I worked together cleaning the glass on the doors as we talked about our families. He then told me that he has a brother in the program at our location. The conversation then turned to our drug of choice and the war stories we endured while using. By the time we stopped talking, all of the work that had been assigned to us was done.

Back at the house, James took me upstairs to the attic. *"This is where my brother sleeps,"* he shared.

"How many people live here," I asked.

"I'm not sure, but my brother stayed here after he completed the program to work."

After putting two and two together, I figured a guy named "Kenny" was who James referred to. He works with the people who clean the church and also lives in the house, but I didn't notice him at the group meeting.

While James and I were getting comfortable, I thought about telling him I had some heroin with me — but I only had seven bags left, so I kept quiet. I decided to lie down until dinner, all while hoping the man who made lunch wasn't making dinner, too.

After dinner, I took a nice, hot shower. I held my head under the nozzle to allow the water to run down the back of my neck. That was the area that held most of my tension and stress. That shower felt **SO** good to me! I *FINALLY* had a moment of peace.

I think the bulk of my stress came from a fear of the unknown and being petrified of failing again. I hadn't accomplished one thing I started in life because I always gave up on myself too soon.

Why, God? Why is it so hard for me to stop using drugs?

I then heard a knock at the door. *"I'm almost done,"* I yelled out.

Well, there went my quiet time! Thoughts of leaving pervaded my mind, but I was well aware of the consequences if I left—and jail was **NOT** an alternative for me!

KNOCK, KNOCK, KNOCK! Again, with the damn knocking!

"Okay, okay! I'm almost done!"

The last few moments of my quiet time were spent with me wondering about the path that I was on. My heart troubled me, while my addiction comforted me. I didn't know how to communicate my pain and how my emotions made me feel. What I desired most was for my father to hold me in his arms and to hear him say, *"It's going to be okay, son."* Tears formed in the corners of my eyes at that moment, but I refused to let them fall. I was not in a place where I could show any signs of feebleness. In reverse, I had no problem expressing the anger I felt because that side of me fed on my hurt and pain and lashed out at every turn. I couldn't deal with my reality, so I self-medicated my emotions when I couldn't express what I felt.

Turned By Grace

I wished that my heart could speak what I could not verbalize. My feelings and emotions were all bottled up inside, wanting to express love and feel the return of the love that eluded my heart.

Jeffrey G. Mitchell, Sr.

CHAPTER FOUR
CONFUSION SETS IN

The evening of my first day, all of the men in the house went to a meeting. There were a few new faces in the crowd *(I guess they were at work when I arrived that morning)*. The meeting was being held in a building around the corner. As we entered, friendly greetings flowed throughout the room. It seemed like a nice place overall.

We made our way to the meeting room on the second floor, where I noticed that only men were present, including about eight of the guys from the house. I quickly discerned that a lot of the other attendees were **NOT** there because of drugs. They didn't look like we did whatsoever.

A man wearing a minister's collar like the one Minister Boyd had on asked everyone to stand to our feet and give God the highest praise. I looked around the room and observed a lot of the men shouting out to God, including my roommate, James. I watched them all in amazement because I could feel the power in the room. I was totally fascinated by what was going on all around me. This was **NOT** the Narcotics Anonymous (NA) meeting I was expecting. As a matter of fact, I didn't think we were in the right place at all. *Maybe the NA meeting was on a different floor…*

I asked the Spanish guy next to me, *"What meeting is **THIS**?"*

He explained, *"This is a men's meeting. Men from the church meet here on Monday nights to discuss men's issues and support the Bishop."*

"The Bishop? Who is that?" I asked.

At that moment, the man in the collar started reading from his Bible from the Book of John 12:25-26:

"He that loves his life shall lose it; and he that hateth his life in this world shall keep it unto life eternal. If any man serves Me, let him follow Me; and where I am, there shall also my servant be: if any man serves Me, him will My Father honor."

By the time the minister finished talking about us "being in the world but not of the world," I was confused about how to do that.

CHAPTER FIVE
DOPE SICK AND SAVED

Soon enough, I fell into the schedule we had to follow while living in the transitional house. Monday through Friday, we attended early morning prayer at the church. On Saturdays, we went at 7:00 a.m. I would often watch and listen to the others guys in the house say a prayer or read a passage of scripture from the Bible. They would then go on to say a few words about how God was helping them to make better decisions in their lives.

(I always sat in the fifth or sixth row from the front. I was fearful of saying anything, especially after James and a few others would speak. They seemed to identify with what the Bible taught...and I didn't.)

There was always some Ministers, Deacons, or Elders with us at the services. I recall there being two Elders who would come with their wives who were Deaconesses in the church.

One morning, I made the mistake of sitting in the front row. One of the Deaconesses asked me to stand and say something. I was so fearful, I cannot even remember to this day what I said. After that experience, I made sure I never sat up front again.

On March 7, 2002, I asked Jesus to be my Savior. Let me back up for just a moment to tell you about *THAT* day...

I awoke "dope sick." I had finished my last bag of heroin the day before, so when it was time to get up for morning prayer, I told the guys to go ahead without me because I wasn't going. I felt flu-like symptoms, so I laid in the bed and started saying stuff like, *"If there is a God, then help me. I keep hearing all of this talk about You and how mighty You are. I also heard that You're a forgiver of sin. Well, here is Your chance to show me! Help me through my sickness."*

You cannot play with God, people! His Word is tried and true!

"Jesus answered and said unto him, 'Verily, verily, I say unto thee: Except a man be born again, he cannot see the Kingdom of God."
~ **John 3:3** ~

Around 9:00 a.m., I heard Minister Boyd come through the front door. I quickly turned on my side, away from anyone passing by. About 20 minutes later, Minister Boyd came up and said, *"I want you to get up and come downstairs to the meeting."* Reluctantly and feeling very sick, I took a shower before I went to the meeting, hoping the shower would make me feel at least a little better, which it did.

After the meeting, we were told we were going to move some furniture for a member of the church. The men in the transitional house do a lot of different kinds of jobs for the people in the church, and our services are often volunteered. I guess that's because the program is funded by the church. So, about six of us went to help move the furniture. One of the younger men named "Joe" was our driver. He was around 19 years old. Any time I used to ride with him, I would tell him to slow down. I couldn't stand the way he drove! I sat in my seat and prayed the whole ride every time I had to ride anywhere with him.

We went to New Brunswick, an area near Johnson Park. When we pulled up to the house, I was the last to exit the van because I knew I wasn't going to be much help to them.

You see, when you are "dope sick," there's not much you **CAN** do. You have flu-like symptoms that pretty much keep you from doing any type of hard, physical work.

My time there consisted of me going back and forth from the van, checking to see how much longer they would be. When someone would ask me why I wasn't helping and explained that we would finish earlier if I did, my response was to walk back to the van and lie down in the back.

Finally, they finished the move! We headed back to the house and had to prepare for Bible Study. I didn't need to shower because I hadn't done any work, so I just washed up and put on a pair of jeans and a sweater. This was to be the first time I would get a chance to see the Bishop — the man I heard about at the men's meeting and the one the guys in the house often spoke about.

When we entered the church, the choir was already singing songs of worship and praise. The Bishop then came out and talked to the congregation. I did my best to tune in to what was being said, but I was distracted from truly hearing the word that was taught that night. Before service ended, Bishop asked, *"Is there anyone who is not saved in this service?"* My right arm shot straight up in the air. I turned and looked at James and asked him accusingly, **"Why did you put my arm up?"** He said, *"I didn't do that!"*

I then heard Bishop say, *"I see that hand up in the back. Come forth, son."*

As I made my way past the other men in my row and down the aisle toward Bishop, the church exploded with applause. Bishop then shook my hand and instructed me to follow one of his Elders. The Elder and I went down the stairs and into a room that was away from the sound of the service that continued upstairs. He asked me, *"Do you believe that Jesus is the Son of God and that He died on the cross for your sins?"*

"Yes."

"Okay," he continued, *"confess your sins to God and ask Jesus to come into your heart."* I did as I was told. After that, he said, **"You are now a son of God!"** He then hugged me and told me that I was going to re-experience my past. Although I didn't really understand what he meant, I replied, *"Okay."* He and I made our way back upstairs to the sanctuary. Service was over, but the guys had stayed behind and waited on me.

That night, when I was trying to go to sleep, it was just as the Elder said; my mind recollected all of the hurt I caused in my life to my family and friends. I felt so bad, I actually started crying…quietly. Then, I thought about how Jesus died for my sins and cried even more. I was simply overwhelmed with all that I was going through. The events of that evening had stimulated my emotions and feelings.

CHAPTER SIX
I WANTED WHAT HE HAD

The morning of Sunday, March 17th, I saw how mighty and magnificent the Lord is. Before then, I never knew that God and Jesus are one and the same, let alone adding in the fact that I was learning about the Holy Spirit, too.

I was up early that morning—at about 4:30 a.m.—lying in my bed thinking about God. I rose and headed to the kitchen from my new room *(I had moved out of the hallway into the bedroom closest to the kitchen, and this room had a door)*. When I changed rooms, "Edward" became my roommate until he suddenly left the program. My early morning routine consisted of me making coffee and going to sit on the back porch to talk to God before everyone else woke up.

The men in the house and I attended two, sometimes three, services on Sundays. The guys who helped out in the Sight and Sound Ministry would also go to a church in Plainfield to assist with setting up the equipment there. *(I helped out a couple of times, but I prefer listening to the Word being preached, even though I didn't fully understand what was being said at the time.)*

As my relationship with God grew, I knew He wanted me to start talking and sharing all that He had done in my life, but I remained nervous about talking in front of people—especially those I didn't know. Plus, after listening to other people say how God had been a blessing to them, I didn't think what I had to say was important or even relevant.

One of my many conversations with God went something like this: *"Look, God: I barely talk when people ask me a question. I **KNOW** You remember when I was little, and my dad used to take me to his mother's house. When grandma would ask me if I wanted something, I shook my head 'yes' or 'no' in reply. She would look at my dad and say, "Jimmy, tell him to **ANSWER** me!" My dad would instruct me to **TELL** grandma 'yes' or 'no.' When she would ask me something else, I would again shake my head in response."* Why would God expect me to suddenly change from that bashful, little boy?

On Tuesdays, we would go to a church in New Brunswick around 11:00 a.m. for a meeting. The meeting at this church was named "Stepping Out of Darkness."

Oddly enough, they did not allow us to attend any NA meetings. I think it's because we were in a Christian program, and NA is not faith-based. I do know that some of the guys had expressed interest in going to NA meetings to Minister Boyd, but he never gave a direct 'yes' or 'no.'

Anyway, later that same Tuesday evening, we would go to Plainfield for another meeting. Deacon Jones would be there sometimes to run those meetings. He would take turns with another person and discuss "New Beginnings." After the evening meeting, we would go to a Bible Study class in the same location but down the hall from where we were. By the time we arrived, they would have already started. Still, I was enjoying Bible Study and learning about the Word. I truly loved it!

By the time we made it back to Perth Amboy, I was always tired. I wanted to take a shower and head straight to bed. I also got a new roommate named "Dan." I am unsure why he didn't share the hallway room with James or why James wasn't able to come into the room with me instead of staying in the hallway. Nonetheless, I soon learned why God placed Dan in my room: He was able to help me better understand what the Bible said.

Dan knew the Bible very well. There were times when we would be seated at the kitchen table downstairs while waiting for Minister Boyd to arrive for our morning meetings, and I would watch Dan and James go back and forth looking up scriptures in the Bible and talking about them. I used to wonder, *"Will I ever get to that point?"*

Jeffrey G. Mitchell, Sr.

CHAPTER SEVEN
THE PROPHET SPEAKS

I recall the day I had my appointment with Middlesex County Social Services to apply for welfare. I already knew to expect $140.00 a month while in the program. Dan and James went that day, too. Out of the money we received, we had to give Minister Boyd $80.00 and could keep the $60.00 for ourselves.

On the ride to Social Services, the other guys and I were looking through the windows of the van at all of the beautiful women walking around. I said to Dan, *"You will definitely get into trouble out here!"* The ride was so short, I didn't even have time to pray for traveling mercies, even though Joe was driving.

Once we entered the building, we had to have a seat and wait on a hard, wooden bench. Joe stuck his head in and told us he would be back to pick us up. James and then Dan was called in for their intake session, and then me.

When I entered the office, I was greeted by a woman who asked me to have a seat. Not long after, a man entered the room and introduced himself. *"Hi. My name is Larry. I will be doing your intake."* He started asking me a series of questions that included what county I was from and if I had ever been on welfare before. As he was filling out the paperwork, recording my responses, he suddenly stopped writing. I thought he fell asleep, as he had his head down like he was taking a nap.

When Larry finally "came to," he looked up at me and said, *"God said that there is a generational curse on your family – on your father's side."* **(He failed to tell me precisely WHAT that curse was, though.)** He went on to say, *"If you do not break this curse, it will then get ten times worse for your children."* When he started telling me about some of the things I had done both as a child and an adult, I was nervous at first. I then thought I was being pranked someway, believing that he received information about me from someone before my intake—that was until he said something about my childhood that **NO ONE** else knew. After that, he went on to say, *"God said to stop playing with Him, asking for help with your addiction. If you don't stop, God said He will lock you up for ten or 15 years, and when you get out, you won't be a man!"* My nervousness grew to outright **FEAR!** Larry looked deep in thought for a moment before he continued. *"There's something about your childhood that God is trying to show me, but I can't seem to see it."*

I knew right then and there that God was trying to tell me that He does exist. He knew me and what I had done as a child. There was **NO** way the man who sat before me could have known *ANYTHING* about my childhood. I was genuinely afraid and ready to leave his office.

By the time my intake was done, I didn't know what to say or think about the experience with Larry. I left the office in a daze and went back out to where the other two men were sitting. I took a seat next to James and just stared at him.

"What's the matter?" James asked.

"Nothing," I replied. *"What kind of questions did that guy ask you?"*

"He just asked me some questions to get state aid," came the response.

I then got up, walked outside away from the building, and looked up at the sky. I asked God aloud, **"Okay, God. You have my attention. What is it that You want from me?"**

Then, a tear rolled down my cheek.

CHAPTER EIGHT
STOP PLAYING WITH GOD!

On the return trip back to the house, I was waiting for any of the other guys to say something—ANYTHING—about their time with Larry that seemed out of place. No one said a thing. As I walked into the house, Dave stopped me and asked, *"Did you meet with Larry?"*

"Why?" I asked.

"Because he called and told me that he prophesied to you."

*"What does **THAT** mean?"* I was truly confused. I followed Dave into the office, and that's when he told me that Larry was a Prophet.

I then understood what Larry meant when he said, *"God said to stop playing with Him."* You see, when I was getting high, I would get into a tub filled with cold water because my heart would start beating really fast after I had used too much heroin. I would then cry out to God, *"Please, do not let me die now!"*—but after I was feeling okay and my heart rate slowed, I would get out of the tub and go right back to using. That behavior went on for at least two more years. I would ask God for help each time, only to go back to using again.

However, what Larry said about a generational curse on my father's side continued to bother me. Why didn't he tell me what it was? How did God expect me to break a curse that I didn't even know existed? I wondered if I should go back and talk to him again. Maybe he would tell me what he meant.

The pain I had inflicted on my loved ones behind my addiction seemed endless:

- I've hurt family members.
- I've disappointed my friends.
- I left my children fatherless.
- I, in essence, left my parents without a son.
- I was estranged from my siblings.

ALL of that anguish…brought on by a drug called "heroin."

I remember my daughter asking me if I loved her when she was little. I would tell her that I did, but she continued to ask me repeatedly, *"Daddy, do you love me?"* I wonder if that was her way of asking me, *"Why are you hurting yourself?"*

My heart was as black as the night's sky, and my pain was locked away deep inside. There was not so much as even a glimpse of light to see in me. How cruel this life was for me! My thoughts were so distorted, even with my good intentions to do what was right. I found myself displaced in doing what was right but always found a way to do what was wrong.

Turned By Grace

Lord, hear me as I plead my heart to You. Why, oh **WHY**, Lord can't I find my way?

CHAPTER NINE
BAPTISM DAY

On March 29, 2002, I was baptized. It was a service I will never forget. It was not planned whatsoever. It seemed as if my life was being guided onto a particular path ever since I first entered the transitional house.

I was enjoying the choir and the selection of songs they were singing. The Bishop then asked the congregation, *"Would anyone who has never been baptized before like to do so now?"* My friend "Bob" looked at me and said, *"Let's go!"*

As we walked toward the altar, Minister Boyd shot us a quick smile. Bob and I were the only two from the house who got baptized that day, but there were a lot of other people getting baptized, too. We were led to the back of the church and then down into the basement where we were told to change into a white robe. As we were changing clothes, the choir continued singing, and the congregants in the sanctuary were clapping and praising God.

While I waited in line for my turn, I watched as the Bishop would whisper something into the ear of the person he was about to dip in the pool of water. As each would come up, I said to myself, *"I don't want to come up the same when he does me."* So, when my turn came, Bishop spoke into my ear. At the same time, I asked God, *"When I come up, please change me. I do not want to be like this anymore or live my life this way any longer."*

After the baptism, Bob and I changed back into our clothes and went back to our seats in the sanctuary. When we passed Minister Boyd, I stopped, hugged him tightly, and thanked him.

That night, when I got on my knees to pray, I thanked God and asked Him for His help. I felt a peace in me unlike anything I've felt before. I was truly a child of God. I accepted Him as my Lord and Savior; in Him, I would learn to trust. I recall soaking my pillow with tears that night. I even placed the cover over my head to cry in silence.

I am grateful that Christ died on the cross for my sins. I want the **WORLD** to know that He is the Lamb of God, who took my sins upon Him. His name is sweeter than any other. He came from Heaven to do on the Earth what no man could have *EVER* done for me. Now, He sits at the right side of God…for you **and** for me.

CHAPTER TEN
THE ENEMY'S PERSISTENT PURSUIT

"Therefore, if any man be in Christ, he is a new creature: old things are passed away; behold, all things are become new."
~ 2 Corinthians 5:17 ~

The following Saturday, as I sat on the back porch drinking my coffee, I told God I needed His help. I desired to do what was right, but my flesh continued to do wicked things. I acted off of my emotions and thoughts of my past, which kept me in a state of discouragement. My mind had yet to catch up with the confession I made of having the Lord as my Savior because I still wanted what my flesh craved.

I started to hear the other guys in the house moving around. It was time to get ready to go to early morning prayer. On this particular day, Deacon Mark would be there. I remember on Saturday, the church wasn't even open for us to enter, and he held prayer right there in front of the church. At first, I thought we were going to go back home, but Deacon Mark told us to grab hands and pray…right there. Not too long after, someone came and unlocked the doors so we could go inside.

Sometimes when we would enter, other ministries would be conducting studies or services, so we would sit in the back where the elderly and children would sit during Sunday services. We would gather around in a circle and talk about our week. On this particular Saturday, we also talked about the baptism service held the Sunday prior. Deacon Mark then read 2 Corinthians 2:5-11:

"But if any have caused grief, he hath not grieved me, but in part: that I may not overcharge you all. Sufficient to a man is this punishment, which was inflicted of many. So that contrariwise ye ought rather to forgive him, and comfort him, lest perhaps such a one should be swallowed up with overmuch sorrow. Wherefore I beseech you that ye would confirm your love toward him. For to this end also did I write, that I might know the proof of you, whether ye be obedient in all things. To whom ye forgive any thing, I forgive also: for if I forgave any thing, to whom I forgave it, for your sakes forgave I it in the person of Christ; lest Satan should get an advantage of us: for we are not ignorant of his devices."

After Deacon Mark finished that reading, he began to discuss being accountable for our actions. He explained that we are to choose righteousness over the needs of the flesh and pray for forgiveness. He then stated, *"We are to look to our Lord for direction. Christ should be our role model in doing right. When we do wrong, we allow Satan a way back in."*

Once our morning session was over, we returned to the house and prepared for a trip to Asbury Park to help with gutting out a bar the church there owned. Dave went with us and, of course, Joe was driving — so you **KNOW** I was praying for traveling mercies from and to our house. Joe's driving was of such a huge concern, we've actually had house meetings about the way he drove.

Jeffrey G. Mitchell, Sr.

The ride to Asbury Park was so much fun. All of us laughed so hard that by the time we arrived, our sides were aching. We laughed and joked with each other, all in the name of fun. We meant no harm to anyone with our jokes. I, for one, was happy for the break away from the house because it helped me relieve some of the pain I held inside.

I remember not having joy or laughter in my life when I was using drugs. Believe me: I was a **miserable** drug addict. Towards the end of my addiction, I had only pain and hurt dwelling within my soul.

Before I knew it, we had arrived at our destination. First, we went to the church and then made our way to the bar. By the time we made it there, it was almost noon. We immediately got to work, pulling up the floor tiles with pry bars, hammers, and floor scrapers. I used to do carpentry work back home, so I was used to using the tools and doing that kind of work.

When we finished for the day, we returned to the church where they had made us some food. We ate until we couldn't eat anymore. It was starting to get dark, so it was time for us to leave.

By the time we made it back to Perth Amboy, I was ready to take a nice, hot shower before bed, but I wasn't the only one who thought a hot shower was a good idea. I went to my room and waited until it was my turn. As I waited, I began to think about how fast the month had gone by…and I hadn't used **any heroin** since my stash ran out.

Enter in the devil and his ploys.

I would often see people in the downtown area of Perth Amboy who were selling drugs. That would cause me to start having recurring thoughts about using again, which started the battle on the inside of me. Imagine for just a moment having something evil in your ear trying to convince you to use. *"Just one bag of heroin won't hurt! Plus, you've been clean for almost a month!"* The enemy's manipulation game was **REAL**!

It was difficult seeing other people using heroin while I walked in the downtown area close to the transitional house. My mind always thought about ways I could get away with using again without getting caught.

I suppose it's best that they had me working and attending the meetings as often as they did. I was hopeful that one day, I would know what life was all about without using any form of mind-altering substance.

When my turn came to take a shower, I hesitated ever so slightly at first. I then decided to go before I totally changed my mind. Although I was tired, I had to prepare myself for the three church services we would likely attend the next day. The way the enemy was trying to get me to use again, I needed **all three** of those services to keep me focused because he was persistent in his pursuit of me!

Jeffrey G. Mitchell, Sr.

CHAPTER ELEVEN
UNDERSTANDING WAS JUST OUT OF MY REACH

The next morning, I awoke early so that I could be the first one to use the iron to press my Sunday clothes. Living with ten other people in the house reminded me of that adage, *"The early bird gets the worm."* On this day, I didn't have coffee on the back porch with God. I hoped He understood that I was tired last night but would be in attendance at church. When I finished ironing my clothes, I made a cup of coffee and sat at the kitchen table to eat breakfast. While I listened to the other guys getting ready for church, I can't begin to explain why I was so excited about going to church. After all, I didn't understand what the preacher said. I did, however, enjoy the songs sung by the choir. One of the songs was called "When the Saints Go to Worship." I felt like crying as I listened to the young lady who sang the solo. Her voice pierced through me, allowing me to feel the power behind each word.

Other than listening to the choir, Dan and I had our attention focused on the women. Whenever they got happy and started jumping, we would get excited watching them. We would nudge each other at the knee and say, *"Look over there."* To be honest, I was so distracted by watching the women, I couldn't hear the Word being preached from the pulpit. I knew that feeding my spirit-man on the Word of God was far more important than what was going on around me, but the fact remained that I just couldn't seem to grasp what *any* of the pastors said.

At the end of service, there was a call for anyone who didn't know Jesus as their Lord to go to the altar and accept Him into their heart. All nonsense I had going on up to that point would cease, as I wanted to see who was going to accept the Lord. Shortly after that call, two of the men from the house left to go set up a table with doughnuts to receive donations for the house. As the church members proceeded out the door, some stopped to look at the selection available and take one or two boxes, along with leaving a donation that would go towards the transitional house.

Once home, the other guys and I would relax and watch whatever sport was on. Football seemed to be the sport of choice for most, but as for me, I liked to relax in my room. By the time we finished three services in a day, I, like most of my brothers in the house, was tired and famished. Sometimes, members of the church would bring us a nice Sunday dinner. I fondly recall Deaconess Mildred's dinners being **VERY** good and enjoyable to eat.

One of the Deacons had a restaurant across the street from the church and, if someone from the house worked over there on any given day, that person would bring something to eat from the restaurant back with them to the house for the rest of us. I would sometimes help by vacuuming the rug or some other light chore. I enjoyed going there whenever the opportunity presented itself. If they asked us, *"Who wants to go to the restaurant and help clean up?"*, I **ALWAYS** said that I would go.

Anyway, as I've stated, a month had gone by since I first arrived at the transitional house. The month of April came, and I started to accept that I needed to be right where I was. Still, I struggled with thoughts about using, especially when I saw it all around me. I suspected some of the guys in the house with me were using, but I chose to stay away from them altogether.

CHAPTER TWELVE
CARRIED BY AN ANGEL

The date was April 17th. It was a day to be spent in Asbury Park again to help with cleaning the bar. When we pulled up to the building, I opened the door and jumped out of the van to stretch my legs while the cleaning tasks were delegated. My job on this day was to work with James to take down the sign that still had the bar's name on it. So, we grabbed a ladder and screwdriver to remove the screws from the sign. The sign had to be 15 feet or more from the ground, causing James to climb to the very top of the ladder to reach the screws and take the sign off the pole as I held the ladder steady from the bottom.

One by one, James unscrewed the screws that held the sign in place. Suddenly, he called down to me and said there was one he couldn't get to come out. I yelled up to him, ***"Try again! Turn it both ways to make sure it's not stripped."***

"It won't come out," he stated matter-of-factly. *"You try!"*

I said to myself, *"That's why I sent you up there; so that I didn't have to climb this ladder!"* What I **SAID**, however, was, "Okay. Come on down, James."

While James and I were on the ground together, I showed him how to properly hold the ladder while I was on it. As I started to climb and then glanced back at James, I noticed he wasn't following my directions. ***"HOLD IT WITH BOTH HANDS!"*** I yelled. I then continued on my climb until I reached the remaining screw. In realizing I was one step too high, I backed down one rung of the ladder and got to the task of releasing the screw. It began to turn with ease, so I was confident that I would be done quickly and on my way back down to the ground…to safety.

All of a sudden, the sign shifted, and the ladder moved right along with it. I thought, ***"OH, NO! I'M GOING TO FALL!*** *I'll hold onto the ladder and go down with it."* I wrapped my hands tightly around the ladder as the sign moved again. That time, the ladder slid, so I quickly resolved to stick to my choice to hang on. Just as I came to grips with my decision, I heard a voice say, ***"JUMP!"*** It was the same voice that told me I was going to be locked up for years. That voice came from deep inside of me again. I released my hands from the ladder and used my legs to push away from the falling pieces of metal.

No sooner than my body cleared the falling ladder, a peace came over me, and everything went in slow-motion. I could see the concern on my brothers' faces. I even had time to look at some people who walked by pointing at me as I fell. Strangely enough, I was not afraid. I felt I was being lowered to the ground by an angel. It seemed as if the fall took forever, but as soon as I was a matter of inches from the ground, it was as if the angel let me go. My heels hit the ground first, and then my feet went from under me. It was then that fear came upon me.

My adrenaline was in overload, though, because I tried to get up. My brothers from the house surrounded me and told me to stay down. Someone had already called the ambulance, but as I laid there, I was fearful and began to worry because my legs were hurting badly and my back was in severe pain.

Dave knelt next to me and said, *"Just lay still. The ambulance is on the way."* I could hear the siren in the distance. *"What hurts on you?"* he asked.

I looked at him and stated, *"My back and legs."*

When the EMTs arrived and asked what happened, I heard a few of the guys explain that I had fallen off the ladder. When the EMTs asked if they knew how high up I was, the shocking reply came: *"About 15 feet or so."*

By the time I arrived at the hospital, my back and legs felt like they were on **FIRE**! I was in a **LOT** of pain. I was placed in a room and waited for the doctor to check on me. After a while, one came in and said, *"How are you feeling? I heard that you fell quite a ways down off a ladder."*

"Yes, I did. The bottom of my feet hurt. I felt a lot of pain when I hit the ground. My back is really hurting me, and I feel sharp pains like I am being stuck with needles all over."

The doctor then said, *"I am going to give you a shot for the pain and take some x-rays."*

After the shot, it wasn't long at all before the pain began to subside. I started to feel really good *(I'm sure I was high on the pain medication)*. When Dave came into the room, he looked at me and said, *"Oh, no."*

"What?" I asked.

"I should have told them you're in a program."

Once the x-rays were done, the hospital released me. I was given pain and muscle relaxer prescriptions to have filled.

I vaguely remember the ride home that day. I was so high, the guys were laughing at me. Whatever the doctor gave me for the pain, I definitely appreciated it because I no longer felt **ANY** pain. By the time we arrived back in Perth Amboy, I had fallen asleep. One of the guys woke me up and said that they needed the prescriptions so that they could have them filled. I recall coming out of my sleep and laughing, saying that I couldn't find them. I then pulled all of my pants pockets inside out and asked, *"Is this it?"*

I don't recall too much of what happened after that…

CHAPTER THIRTEEN
70% WAS MY NEW NORMAL

I may have slept like a baby that night, but when I awoke the next morning, my back was hurting something terrible. When I tried to get out of bed, the bottom of my feet screamed not to even try it. Dan was very thoughtful and brought a cup of coffee to me in the room. *"How are you feeling?"*

"Hurting, bro." I took the pain pill and muscle relaxer with my coffee and laid there while the rest of the guys went to morning prayer. About a half an hour passed, and I tried to get up to go to the bathroom. The sharp pain remained in my legs and back, and my fingers were tingly and felt kind of numb. A new pain joined the bunch: My neck felt as if it was being pinched…**hard**.

I managed to make it to and from the bathroom and immediately laid back down in my bed. At that moment, I cried out to God. *"Why, God? I know that I am not doing all that I should be doing here, but I thought I was trying!"* I got depressed and stopped having my morning coffee time with God on the back porch. I also couldn't do any work, which had some of the guys thinking that I was just faking my injuries.

About three days went by, and my pains were not getting any better. Pains continued to shoot through my back and legs, and my arms were tingling as if being stuck with needles. When Minister Boyd came, I asked to speak with him.

"What seems to be the problem?" he inquired.

"I've been taking the medication that the hospital prescribed, but I feel worse. They just gave me a shot of something to help my pain and sent me home. I think I need to see a doctor or someone who can explain to me why I still have so much pain in my back and legs."

An appointment was made for me with a chiropractor. The doctor took his own x-rays and discussed my level of pain. Once he read the x-rays, he explained the cause of my incessant pain. "*Your spine is out of place in three sections: your cervical, thoracic, and lumbar. Your lumbar 3 has shifted and is pinching your nerves. Your thoracic 4 shifted, and your cervical 7 moved out of line with your neck.*"

At least **THAT** doctor explained to me what happened as a result of my fall. He also said, however, that I may never be 100% again and that he could get me to about 70% normalcy. He went on to say that he wanted to see me three times a week and check on my progress after the first month. Initially, I was upset because I didn't come to the program hurt, yet the doctor said I might have to live with back problems for the rest of my days.

Dan was my driver that day. I noticed that he would talk to a lot of women we saw. He acted like we weren't in a program! On the way to the chiropractor's office, he was talking to some girl on a corner. I said to him, "*Look, man. We have to go. You'll have to get her number some other time. I need to go see this chiropractor."* When he looked over at me, I said, *"What are you going to do?* **Ask her out for a date?** *Look, Dan; you are in a* **program**. *What lies are you telling her?"* He started laughing, and so did I. He knew he was caught.

Dan and I stopped on the way home to get something to eat. My mom and godmother sent me money, even though we were not supposed to have anything extra above the monthly stipends given by the county. I lied and told them they could send money, so they would send $25.00 or $50.00 at a time in a letter or card. On Wednesdays, we were given a couple of hours to shop downtown. As a matter of fact, we were scheduled to go shopping later that same day after we got home. We would shop in groups — which helped me a **LOT** because I didn't want to use drugs anymore, and I was exposed to areas where they were still selling drugs.

CHAPTER FOURTEEN
ONE-ON-ONE TIME WITH ADDICTION'S VOICE

Later that night, after the visit to the chiropractor, the guys and I went to a New Beginnings meeting. "Allen" — one of the other guys in the program — asked me to borrow ten dollars. I explained to him that I spent what I had already when we went downtown shopping. He asked again, pleading:

"Come on, man. I'll pay you back."

I could see that he was using again, so I flat out told him "No."

While we were in the meeting, my old friend "addiction" decided to pay me a visit. I was wondering where he went... I knew it was my addiction talking in my ear because I could distinguish between the voice that said, *"I'm going to lock you up"* and *"JUMP!"* when I was on the ladder. That voice came from **INSIDE** of me. Now, however, my addiction was trying to set me up to use again. He knew I was in pain because of the fall. He also knew the medication I was taking wasn't really helping to ease that pain. My addiction told me, *"If only you had a bag of heroin, you would be okay."*

So, there I sat in the meeting, having a one-on-one conversation with my addiction. You see, when Allen asked me for some money, my addiction said, *"Give him $20.00 and let him go get it. Then, you won't have to worry about being seen doing it. And I'll take that pain right away after you get that heroin in you. I will make **ALL** of your pains go away."*

I responded, *"You just need to shut up right now! I am **NOT** getting high anymore. **Leave me the hell alone!**"* — which he did…for a little while.

As we prepared to settle down for the night, I found myself very frustrated behind Allen asking me for money. My thoughts [addiction] were trying to convince me that *"no one will know and it will help you deal with the pain you are feeling in your back and legs."* I was actually sitting there trying to justify me using again! At the time, it had been nine weeks and six days since the last time I used heroin.

I looked over at Dan, who was still awake and otherwise busy with looking at some girly magazine. I didn't want to bother him with my problem, but I needed to talk to someone. My "problem" was not letting me have any peace.

"Hey, Dan. I need to talk to you," I began.

"What's the matter?" he asked.

I looked at him square in his eyes and said, *"I am thinking about using. My thoughts are trying to give me justification for doing it."*

"Is it because of the pain you're in?"

I had to be honest with him. "That's one reason, but on the way to the meeting tonight, Allen asked to borrow some money. You know like I know why he wanted it. While we were at the meeting, I was in a battle with my addiction. I cannot tell you one thing that was talked about because my addiction spent the entire time trying to manipulate me to use. Man, I felt that spirit of addiction that's on Allen. That same spirit is trying to get me to use, too."

Without hesitation, Dan said, "*Let me show you something.*" He put his magazine down, grabbed his Bible, and turned to the Book of Joshua. He read chapter 24, verses 14 through 15 aloud:

"Now, therefore, fear the LORD, and serve Him in sincerity and in truth: and put away the gods which your fathers served on the other side of the flood, and in Egypt; and serve the LORD. And if it seems evil unto you to serve the LORD, choose you this day that ye will serve; whether the gods which your fathers served that were on the other side of the flood, or the gods of the Amorites, in whose land ye dwell: but as for me and my house, we will serve the LORD."

Dan then tried to explain that passage of scripture to me by saying, *"I think God wants you to make a decision* **TONIGHT**: *Are you going to go back and be in bondage to heroin or are you going to believe God has something better for your life than being addicted to drugs and having to live in bondage?"*

After Dan finished, I thanked him. I was feeling better and knew I had some soul-searching to do. I desperately wanted to know what it felt like not to want to get high anymore.

"**LORD**, *may I serve You, for You're the vine that nourishes the fruit that clings to the branches of faith, which brings forth the fruit of the vine, whose miracles shall be seen in trials and tribulations, which brings forth the fruit of righteousness in God. For You're the sun that gives life and strength, but also, You're the shade that covers and shields, for I rest in You yielding righteous fruit in its season."*

CHAPTER FIFTEEN
JEFF "THE COMPLAINER"

The following morning, I was up early again. For a while, I had stopped meeting God for coffee on the back porch because I felt depressed about falling and had a hard time dealing with my emotions. On this morning, I sat with Him and asked, *"God, why did You allow me to fall from that ladder? Even though I knew You were there to make sure nothing seriously bad happened to me, I still felt abandoned by You. I was trying to get to know You. I asked You to come into my life. I was baptized and started to pray to You. I read my Bible, even when it made no sense to me. I still read Your Word, hoping soon that You would teach me the Word of God."*

There was no response at that time, but I did feel better taking the time to pour my heart out to God in the stillness of the early morning.

It was soon time to head over to early prayer service. When we arrived, I managed to work through my nervousness and read from the Book of Psalms 41:1-9. I then thanked God and quickly sat back down.

As we left the church, I saw Larry passing by the house. A few of the guys stopped to talk with him. He then focused his attention on me. *"How are you feeling?"*

"I'm okay. My back still hurts, and my legs still have sharp pains in them when I walk."

He responded, *"I want you to ask **GOD** what to do."*

After spending a few more minutes with Larry and the guys, I went inside the house to do my chores. When I was done, I went and sat in the back yard and asked God, *"What should I do now about me being hurt? I did not come to this program with a bad back, so why would You want me to leave here like this?"* Before I could receive a response, Dan came to the door and said, *"Minister Boyd is here. Come in for group."* I walked back into the house and went upstairs to my room to get my notebook.

Minister Boyd's group session was about "The Complainer." I could see the eyes of everyone looking around the room. I imagine each one thought of the other, *"He must be talking about **YOU**!"* The reality of the situation was that all any of us needed to do was look in a mirror, and we would see the definition of a 'complainer' staring back at us.

Minister Boyd explained that "The Complainer" is the ultimate victim—one who never seems to get a break in life and believes the world is against him. When he used the term "Drama Queen," everyone laughed. He went on to explain that a Drama Queen:

- Is never understood.
- Is never listened to.
- Always complains about some illness.
- Always asks, **"WHY ME?"**

> Is driven by negative emotions.

I "saw myself" in some of those attributes.

After group, Minister Boyd delegated our duties for the day. I and some of the other guys were assigned the task of helping out some of the members of the church. On that day, we helped to clean up someone's yard. I tried to do some of the light work when we went out, but most of the time, I stayed in the van and talked to God. I would look up at the clouds and express myself to Him, letting Him know how I was feeling that day.

The following day, I was scheduled to go to court for when I got caught. Dave was going with me to let the judge know I did find and enroll in a program. I also asked God if I should consult with a lawyer and ask about my situation because I didn't think it was fair. I knew I entered the program because of my drug problem, but I surely didn't want to leave with a back injury!

Wow! I had to laugh at myself. Look at me **COMPLAINING!**

I said a prayer:

"God, help me to look at the character defects in my life. I want to change my ways, but I am going to need Your help to shed off the old man so that I may walk as a newly-created man in Christ. Thank You, Jesus. **Amen.***"*

CHAPTER SIXTEEN
THE ENEMY IS ALWAYS CLOSE

"I beseech you, therefore, brethren, by the mercies of God, that ye present your bodies a living sacrifice, holy, acceptable unto God, which is your reasonable service."
~ Romans 12:1 ~

I lay before you God, in faith, to be consumed by the fire of the Holy Ghost; a living sacrifice, that ye may burn and cleanse my corrupt soul. Be ye swift and powerful, Holy Spirit. Separate with the fire from Heaven. Free me from my past life. Be merciful, my Lord, as I desire to serve as a living sacrifice. My past, however, is not yet fully dead. The stench of my flesh is looking for me in a place I no longer care to be kept. No matter how hard I try to escape my flesh, it finds me.

Why is that, Lord? A spirit attaches itself to me, causing me considerable harm, my Lord, because that which it makes me do is only pleasing to my flesh but harmful to my soul. The closeness that I desire with my Lord is in my bones like the marrow. I desire to be filled with the Holy Ghost. Fire from Heaven above is what I seek.

Although the enemy is close to me, I will never stop believing greater is He that is in me. My soul cries out for change, but my flesh continues to battle for dominance. My God, my Deliverer, to whom I belong; let not my mind and flesh do what is pleasing to this world. Consider my heart in the newness of Christ and how it now feels about the evil of this world.

At one time, my heart was troubled with the cares of this world — darkened by the pain it felt and the hurt that waded in it from life's situations. But my God, who is merciful and my refuge, placed me within His bosom and showed me a love I never knew before. He showed me **AGAPE** love.

Abba, Father: I do so want to be filled from the crown of my head to the very soles of my feet with Your presence. I long for the Holy Ghost inside of me, shut up in my bones, teaching me all things about Jesus, and bringing me the remembrance of the Word of God. My flesh is so caught up in this world and how I think. My God, who is the architect of life itself, who is a deliverer from things of the past; I lay my life before you, troubled by this spirit. Countless times, I tried to break free from this, only to return to my flesh and its evil thoughts. So, after trying on my own and failing, I beseech You, My God. Intercede on my behalf.

Tell me Lord: Why did You reveal my enemy unto me, only to let him gain control over me? My heart is longing to do right, but I can't see past my flesh. When I call for help, the enemy is in my camp, singing and dancing a victory chant. My esteem is low as I look for deliverance.

The feeling of defeat causes me great distress, and my help seems far away from me. A feeling of inept is upon me, unable to continue the fight or wish to do battle with this enemy any longer. How does one keep his appearance as a man of God after being defeated by his adversary? My battle cry is at a murmur. Not even I believe, so who would follow me into battle?

~~~~~~~~~~

My son, all that I have shown you was not for you. I know the adversary all too well and why the attacks on you are so vile. He is out to destroy a generation and has declared war on you. You have seen what few wonder about. Go back and think it through. I would never show you defeat without a way out.

Remember who was there? I showed you who he battled in the past and who was to battle him in the future, but it is the present that matters now to whom I have given the victory.

He can only win the war if you give up. Yes, a beating was given to you and defeat has rested in your mind, but now is not the time to pass the battle to another. Encourage yourself and let not your enemy take the spoils of this war. I've shown you what you are up against and the spoils of this war he is after. I've also shown you he is not of your world.

When he had his hands on you, manipulating and controlling you towards the end, whose name was called from your mouth to free you from the grip of your enemy? **JESUS'** name!

CHAPTER SEVENTEEN
PLEASE DON'T LEAVE ME, LORD

The day finally arrived when I had to go to court for when I was arrested in December 2001. I was hopeful that because I was already in a program, they would allow me to remain with Dave and the guys. Dave and I were scheduled to leave immediately after morning prayer.

I prayed and asked God to help me because I did **NOT** want to spend three years in anyone's jail. I asked God for favor with the judge and prosecutor. After my prayer, I waited on the front porch for Dave.

To get to the courthouse, Dave and I had to take the train. Once at the station, he asked me if I was nervous. I told him, *"I woke up nervous, but after talking with God and asking Him to give me favor with the judge, I'm not nervous now!"* He and I shared a good laugh. It turns out Dave is not that bad of a person at all when he is outside of the confines of the program. He told me that he went through the program, having spent six months at the transitional house *(it has since changed, and participants are mandated to complete 13 months)*. He went on to say that Minister Boyd asked him to stay on and help out, placing him in a position of being our counselor.

THAT explained the boisterous laughter I often heard coming out of the office when Dave and Minister Boyd were in there together.

When we pulled into the Elizabeth train station, we exited and walked to the courthouse. As I climbed the steps, I prayed, *"God, please don't leave me here."*

Well, I walked out of the courthouse that day! The judge seemed pleased that I was in a program. Even the prosecutor wished me well. On the return trip home, I was thrilled. I started to believe in myself again and that it was time to see that rainbow in my life.

That night, I made up my mind to seek after God, but I had a question to ask Him: **WHY ME?**

So many of my friends were dead or had stints in and out of prison. Clearly, He saved me for something, leaving me to ask: **WHY?** I asked God to show me His will for my life. No longer did I wish to live the way of the world. I desired to be who He created me to be. He is my Creator and I, His creation. Since He created me in His image, I asked Him to show me what He created me for.

That following Saturday, a couple of us were scheduled to clean a church member's yard. After spending some time cutting and raking the yard, the homeowner offered us something to drink. She then offered us some books she had on her dining room table. Paul was the first one over there looking at them. I spent some time in her living room viewing her family photos, seeing if I knew anyone in them *(the woman lived not far from my parents' home)*.

Paul called me over to the table and said, *"This book is for you, Jeff."* I looked at it and read its title: *God's Calling*. It appeared to be a daily devotional book, so I placed it in the van. I wanted to be sure not to leave it behind. After we finished our drinks, we made the trip back to the house. Oddly enough, I didn't see anyone I knew while out; odd because I was very close to home.

That night, I read the devotional that Paul gave me. I started on May 18th. It talked about prayer and how prayer changes things. It also said prayer should turn into praise.

The following morning, I awoke early for my coffee time with God. That morning, I also read from *God's Calling*. I made it a point to do my ironing the night before so that I could spend more time with God this particular morning. I always enjoyed the peace I had while sitting on the back porch and telling God what I felt and how it affected me. I would also let Him know when someone or something bothered me.

At church, something different happened to me that day. When Dan nudged my knee to get my attention to look at the women in the church from time to time, I asked him to stop. I explained why:

"I want to hear the Word that's being preached."

At first, Dan got upset with me. *"What about your girl up there; the one you're always looking at? What, you don't want to look at her anymore?"*

I replied, *"Come on, man. Not now. Let me hear what is being said."*

From that day, while I was still distracted at times by the beautiful women in the church, I was also starting to hear and understand the words being preached from the Bible. I even started taking notes and could find the passages that were being read!

The enemy didn't like that at all. As sure as the night turns to day, he came for me.

CHAPTER EIGHTEEN
TEMPTATION'S KNOCK

One day, after Minister Boyd's group session, I was assigned to be Bob's escort to the dentist's office. As stated previously, we had to go places together so that we could hold each other accountable for our actions. So, after our chores were done, Bob and I made the trip to the dentist.

When we arrived, I noticed that Bob was more interested in the person who lived in the apartment above the dentist's office. I could see that the dentist was on the first floor, but Bob was ringing the bell to the second floor.

"What are you doing?" I asked. "The dentist's office is downstairs. Why are you ringing that doorbell?"

"A friend lives here," he said. "I want to go up and say hi to her."

Well, he definitely got the "high" part right. When his friend finally came and answered the door, I knew right away that she was a crack addict. Bob tried his best to get me to go upstairs with them.

"Look, I am **NOT** going into her house. I am going back home. You can stay if you want, but I'm leaving – with or without you." I started to walk away, heading back to the house. By the time I made it around the corner, Bob had caught up with me.

"*Man, I just wanted to see if you would have gone up with me,*" he stated.

I was very firm with what I said next. "*Do **NOT** put me in a situation like that ever again.*"

Bob was from Perth Amboy. I had noticed that when we were allowed to walk to the waterfront, he would try and stop by someone's house. He would call out to the guys and me, "*Wait up! Let me say hello to my family.*" Most of us never waited. I had no desire to meet or even know whose house he was spending time at.

As we approached the house after the dentist office visit, Bob asked me, "*Are you going to say anything about what happened earlier?*"

I looked at him with a bit of disdain and said, "*No.*" I kept my word and didn't tell, but I **also** knew not to go **anywhere** else with him alone. I had enough difficulty fighting my own addiction as it was.

The rest of that day, I didn't speak to Bob. When we *were* in the presence of one another, I was cordial with him, as if nothing happened. He knew I was struggling with not using while in the program, so I didn't understand why he thought our going into a crack addict's house was a good idea.

CHAPTER NINETEEN
THE ADDICTIVE SPIRIT KNEW ME

The last week of May was approaching. I had been clean for 78 days. Never had I had that much clean time since my addiction. That is why I was so upset with Bob when he pulled that mess with me.

You see, it was hard for me to see people using out in the streets. I tried not to look when I saw them, but it was hard not to notice. I was still drawn to that old, familiar spirit. So, when I saw that spirit of addiction on them, I knew it wanted to jump back in me. I realized that I was one step away from re-embracing my addiction at any time.

I knew that addictive spirit—and it knew me...well. It was not going to let me loose that easily. I battled with him daily, as I watched some of the guys in the house getting high. As for me, I had my own fight to win. I was holding onto Jesus so tightly, the spirit of addiction kept its distance—while still letting me know it was ever so close. It taunted me and whispered, *"I'm here if you want to come back."*

When I was out there in my addiction, it started isolating me from my family and the few friends I still had. I was the only one out of my siblings who still used heroin. In 2000, my younger sister and brother had stopped and were going to NA meetings. But me? I couldn't stop using. At one point in my addiction, it had me thinking I was "the special one." It said to me, *"They stopped using because they got scared, but you are like a god! You can do this!"* That thing had me fooled into thinking I was able to use and nothing would ever happen to me!

I was so caught up in my addiction, nothing else in life mattered to me. I remember the day my godmother (who is my mom's best friend) said to me, *"Your mother and I are praying to God that you get locked up."* Both of them knew I was too far gone to get help for myself. I was at the point where my addiction was saying, *"You've lived long enough. Look at all of these young men dying at an early age. Your friends are either dead or locked up. At the age of 40, that's long enough to live."*

I hope you understand by now why I hold onto Jesus so tight. I heard about jail experiences and death while I was in my addiction. I hopped from program to program. The difference between those and the transitional house I was in was that none of those other programs said a thing about **JESUS**. I've been to Hell. I've walked and talked with death. One day, God said, ***"I want him now."***

I was hopeful that the new program would show me how to live life again—without the use of **ANY** form of mind-altering substance.

Drugs were here before me, and surely, they will be here after me. I have a choice today and a fighting chance to save my life, all because of **JESUS**.

CHAPTER TWENTY
FOCUSED AND FREE

The date was May 31st. It was a pretty good day. Allen was no longer in the house with us, but I was hopeful that he would find another program sooner than later. Still, I knew from experience that once the addiction grabs hold of you, it's hard to just **STOP** on your own.

I said a prayer for Allen in church that morning. I also prayed for my family. My mom and godmother were coming to see me the following day. I felt kind of nervous, yet happy at the same time. I was excited about seeing my family. Even though we were not supposed to leave Perth Amboy, I had already made up in my mind to leave and go home. I had a six-hour pass and had no plans of hanging out in the area.

I recall a time when I was intimidated by simply hearing some of the other guys pray in church. It never ceased to amaze me that some of those same men were not who I came to know once outside of the church's doors. Their lifestyle didn't match up.

God is concerned about what's in our heart; not what's said around people. He wants to hear from our heart through our prayers and thanks to Him. The first time I read aloud during service was when I read Psalms 41. After that, I would talk to God from my heart, letting Him know how I felt and what I was going through. I spoke to Him on the back porch or in early prayer. I poured out my heart to Him, and He started answering me back through His Spirit. He gave me specific instruction:

"Listen to what they say to Me in prayer."

So, I started truly listening to what was being said by my brothers who lived in the house. I then watched them do the opposite of what they said.

I learned to embrace God as my Best Friend. I would sit and talk with Him about how I felt and about someone or something that was bothering me. I was even upset a couple of times when I would talk to Him. If my emotion at the time was anger, I would express it to Him—but not *AT* Him. Thankfully, there were more feelings of joy. I am grateful today for the relationship I have with the Father.

So, the day marched on. I was overjoyed about my family's visit the next day, but I had first to make it through *that* day. Our duties encompassed helping a lady put some of her belongings into a storage unit. When we arrived, she already had a lot of the items packed up in boxes, which helped make the job easier.

Not long after we arrived, Dan came over to me and said, *"Jeff, look at her!"*

"Yeah, she is nice-looking—and I know her," I replied.

"*FOR REAL?*" I could hear the excitement in Dan's voice.

"*Yeah. She's about a year older than me, but I remember her from school.*"

"*Introduce me, Jeff!*"

I walked over to Kelly and said, "*Hi.*"

She replied, "*I thought maybe you didn't remember me because you didn't speak earlier.*"

"*I remember you from school,*" I confirmed. In my thoughts, I also remember I used to like her, but nothing ever happened between us. Kelly and I talked for a while and then I mentioned to her that one of the guys helping with the move wanted to be introduced to her. "*Is that okay with you? I wanted to ask you first.*" She said yes, so I made the introduction and walked away to let the two of them talk.

Once all of her things were loaded into the rental truck, we drove to the storage unit to unload and stack it all. Just as we were about to leave, Kelly came over to me and said, "*I thought YOU might have wanted to talk to me.*"

I smiled at her and said, "*I would have liked to, but right now, I need to focus on my recovery.*"

"*I understand and can respect that. It's great that you want to get your life back in order.*"

This conversation caused me to wonder, so I asked, *"What about Dan?"*

"He's not my type," she stated matter-of-factly.

In a way, I was glad because Dan was a dog. He thought **every** girl liked him. On the way home, Dan went on and on about how he was going to call Kelly and hook up with her. I laughed and said, *"Okay, man. Good for you."*

CHAPTER TWENTY-ONE
FOND MEMORIES

When we got back to the house, I took a quick shower. We were all going to New Brunswick to hear a Jazz band. At first, I thought we were going to a club, but it turned out to be a theater. During intermission, I saw a lady I knew but couldn't remember where from. From where we were seated, I could see her…and I think she noticed me gazing in her direction. I was sitting next to James, and even he noticed.

"*Why do you keep looking over there? Don't you see that big dude sitting next to her?*" James asked.

"*Yeah, but she's looking over at me, too! I know her from somewhere, but I can't remember from where,*" I replied.

After the show and as we were leaving, I saw her at the door. I stopped her and asked, "*Do I know you? You look like someone I met before.*" When she told me her name, I said, "*Oh! Okay! I used to come over your house when I was in elementary school. I had to be about ten years old. I would come over to your house with my best friend to see your younger sister.*" Once she and I put two-and-two together, I asked how her family was and to tell her sister I said hi.

As the guys and I made our way back to the van, I explained to Dan that after my friend and I would leave her house, she would always give both of us a kiss on the cheek. I knew there was something familiar about her that kept me looking in her direction.

That night, as I laid in my bed, I thought about how I stared at her and couldn't stop looking her way. I even made the man she was with uncomfortable, to the point that he said something to me while I was speaking with her at the exit. Once she remembered that I used to come over to her mother's house to see one of her younger sisters, she explained to him that I was a friend of the family and told him to stop acting jealous. I see now that it could have ended a different and very wrong way.

CHAPTER TWENTY-TWO
86 DAYS CLEAN

As I sat on the back step sipping on my hot coffee and looking up at the clouds, I thought about how beautiful it was to be up early and appreciate the quietness of being alone to talk with God. It was so peaceful, and the air was so sweet at that time of the morning. I longed for that time with God. Everyone in the house was still asleep, and morning prayer wasn't until 7 a.m. on Saturdays. I was in a good place: happy and ready to see my children and family.

There was a problem I had, though. I couldn't release the thoughts that plagued me about the harm I had done and what I put my parents and children through—from my oldest daughter to my youngest son. I cried a lot in my room at night because of the hurt I caused and the pain I put my family through.

God, how is it that You can forgive me, but I am having a hard time forgiving myself? My heart is feeling the pain that I caused to so many due to my addiction. Help me, Lord, to forgive myself. I carry the hurt in my heart and can't seem to forgive myself for what I did to them.

I heard my brothers begin to move around the house, so I ended my one-on-one time with God and thanked Him for listening to me.

At the door of the church, Deacon Mark was waiting for us. Instead of going into the church for prayer, he took us to breakfast at a place downtown. We sat in some booths in the back and talked and listened to Deacon tell us about all the different places he had been. It was kind of him to take us out that day, and we all thanked him.

Once back at the house after breakfast, we did our chores. My nervousness about leaving and going home remained. I thought about getting caught, but I just wanted to see my children. Around noon, my mom and godmother arrived. Dave was on the front porch when I got into the car. My mom waved to him and asked, *"How is he doing?"*

Dave responded, *"He's okay."*

As soon as we pulled off, I said, *"Let's go **home**."*

Both of them were obviously surprised because they asked in unison, ***"You can leave?"***

"Yes."

So, we started the trip towards home. On the way, I told them about the program and how much work they had us doing for members of the church. I explained about the New Beginnings and Stepping Out of Darkness meetings, and about the men's meeting on Mondays. I ended with, *"By the time my day is over, I just want to **sleep**!"*

My mom asked, *"How's your back?"*

"It's still bothering me, but not as much as when it first happened." I also told them about morning prayer and how I am learning the Bible and about Jesus.

My godmother asked the burning question that I know **both** of them had: *"How long has it been since you last used, Jeff?"*

With pride, I told her, *"Today makes 86 days clean!"*

Both of them were very happy for me.

By this time, we had arrived at Joan's house—my children's mother. She had three of my children, and I had custody of my two oldest. I got out of the car and hugged and kissed my children and Joan. As we started to leave after our visit, my little girl said, *"I miss you, daddy,"* and hugged me tightly in the car. When we arrived at my parents' house, my mom said she was going to cook something on the grill for us to eat. Joan and I decided to take the kids to the park, so I told my mom we would be back later.

As Joan and I watched the kids play, she and I talked. She asked how I was doing, and I said, *"Okay."* I knew at that moment I no longer felt the same about us. I went on to say, *"I need some time. I am just getting to know who I am."* She got upset with me, so I walked over to the swings and played with my children.

Turned By Grace

When we made it back to my parents' house, I had a serious conversation with Joan. *"Do you remember how I would come home from being away at one of those detox places and, as soon as I would come to see you and the kids, you would start complaining to me about what I wasn't doing? Please, I didn't need you to remind me of that mess. I already knew what I wasn't doing. Still, you used it to beat me down. When I had enough of you putting me down and making me feel like less than a man, I would use that as an excuse to stop and buy myself a bag of heroin on the way home, just so I could get you out of my head."*

I could tell the conversation was making her uneasy, but I had to speak up, so I continued.

"Look, Joan. I am not blaming you, but you never gave me a chance to breathe before you would tell me all of what I don't do. Today, I feel good and am not ready to talk about what I am going to do now. I just want to be in today. I can only handle today because tomorrow isn't here yet. Please let me live in today." I knew right then I was no longer going to be in a relationship with Joan once I completed the program.

Before my return trip to the transitional house, I spent time talking to my oldest children—the ones who saw me in all of my addiction. The relationship with my oldest daughter wasn't good at all because I was not a father to her nor my son. My parents raised them in their house. I was just "there" in a zombie-like personality. I had no feelings; neither did I care about anything except where my next bag of heroin was coming from.

Jeffrey G. Mitchell, Sr.

The six-hour pass seemed to **fly** by. Feelings of sadness begin to overtake me, but I was also ready to go back to the house. I found that I started having those old, familiar feelings of when I used to get high in my parents' house. I needed to be on my way. I actually felt more comfortable back in Perth Amboy. There was an indescribable feeling of being in a secure place that enveloped me there. I said my goodbyes to my children and hugged my dad.

CHAPTER TWENTY-THREE
IT FEELS GOOD TO GIVE

When I made it back to the transitional house, I knew that was where I belonged. I had started to receive the help I was so desperately in need of. It was a combination of everything: being with my brothers in the house, going to the meetings and church, and early prayer. I even found out that when we go out to work and help the people in the church, I was giving back. That felt good to me. I helped someone who was in need, without the expectation of anything in return. That didn't stop me from working as if I was getting paid!

That night before I went to bed, I got on my knees and thanked God for letting me be and stay in the house. I had been through a few different programs, but none were like that one *(I felt alone and ashamed in those other programs)*. At the transitional house, I felt the love of God. Plus, a lot of church members were very nice and all the leadership I met transferred the love of Christ to me.

I started to believe that God was very intentional in bringing me to the house. I began to feel like I was supposed to be there, getting to know God for myself intimately.

I remember about a couple of years before entering the house, I went to a methadone clinic. My counselor there was an evangelist, and he asked me one day to come hear him preach. When I asked where and he told me the church's name, I knew exactly where it was because my mother and godmother were members there. Not only had I been there before, but I also did my drugs in their bathroom. At that point in my life, if I had to go **ANYWHERE**, I had to be high, or I would not have been able to sit still. Anyway, I decided to go the night the evangelist preached and, after service, he said to me, *"Go over there* [which was about six feet away from him] *and say, 'Thank You, God,' over and over again."* I did as I was told, feeling nothing.

So, there I was, years later—on my knees and thanking God.

I want to pause in my writing to thank my dad, mom, and godmother for never giving up on me and for praying for me. I am learning that when you give up on yourself, you let the enemy have victory over you. Now, I thank God—the One who had other plans for my life. Even when I couldn't begin to envision myself off the drugs…even when I started to believe the enemy's lies that said my life was over at the age of 40, somebody took the time to pray for me. At the time of this writing, I will celebrate my 41st birthday in two months—saved and seeking the **LORD**!

HALLELUJAH! HALLELUJAH! HALLELUJAH TO THE LAMB OF GOD!

I now know why I read Psalms 41 during early morning prayer that day. Reader, hear the Word of the Lord:

"Blessed is he that considered the poor; the LORD will deliver him in times of trouble. The LORD will preserve him and keep him alive, and he shall be blessed upon the Earth: and thou wilt not deliver him unto the will of his enemies."
~ Psalm 41:1-2 ~

AMEN! Thank You, Jesus!

Now that You have me where you want me, speak Lord! Speak to me!

"Draw nigh to God, and He will draw nigh to you. Cleanse your hands, ye sinners; and purify your hearts, ye double-minded."
~ James 4:8 ~

CHAPTER TWENTY-FOUR
GOD SAID, "STOP DOING THAT!"

Another weekend had come and gone. The day was Monday, and I had an appointment with Larry at Social Services. I was unsure of the reason why I had to go back there. I was also thinking about asking Minister Boyd if I could see a lawyer because my back was **still** bothering me. I felt bad about wanting to sue, but I also didn't want to end up with a back problem for the rest of my life without being able to afford the care.

The week prior, I visited the library and did some research on the spine. Earlier that week, I also tried to see how much I could do before discomfort settled in my back. I tried lifting weights on the weight bench and light exercise. While at the library, I read that damage to the spine may only be temporary, but injuries could lead to some degree of permanent disability since the nerves' pathways help control many of the body's actions and functions.

I prayed and asked God to help me make the right decision. I didn't want to sue the program, but it goes without saying I didn't have a problem with my back when I walked through their doors.

James was my buddy that day for the walk over to Social Services. He told me that he wanted to ask Minister Boyd if he could go home for a day. I told him they might not let him go for the **WHOLE** day, but to ask for a short visit. He was determined to leave the house for an entire day. I went on to explain that if he left, they might not allow him back into the program. *"Are you willing to take that risk, just to see whoever it is that you want to leave here for? Well, I hope she is worth it because if they tell you no and you leave anyway, I can't see them letting you come back,"* I said.

Once we arrived at the office, I checked in with the receptionist and had a seat. While we were waiting, James asked me if he could borrow some money.

"No. If you leave, I won't be the one helping you. I'm not going to say anything to anyone, but I won't give you the money to leave," I said sternly.

On my way in to see Larry, I turned and looked back at James. I wondered whether or not I should help him. As I walked into Larry's office, he asked me how I was doing. I told him okay but that I planned on asking Minister Boyd to see a lawyer because I was still having problems with my back. He then said, *"I am not trying to tell you what to do, Jeff, but let God handle it for you."* Larry didn't know that I had already consulted God. **GOD** was the reason I went to the library to do my research in the first place.

Once the small talk was over, Larry got down to the reason for my visit. *"I called you down here because I need your signature on some papers."* While I signed them, Larry suddenly said, *"God wants you to stop doing what you are doing in the shower."*

I lifted my head, and my hand stopped writing midstride. *"What did you say?"*

"God said to stop doing that thing you do when you are in there taking a shower."

I started to laugh uncontrollably! I even slid out of the seat!

Larry said, *"He shows me these things."*

That made me laugh even harder! After we **both** stopped laughing, I asked Larry if he had the gift of speaking in tongues. He said he did and wondered why I asked. *"Oh, because while I am in church, I can hear people talking in tongues. It sounds funny, but I am drawn to it whenever I hear it. Does God give you that gift or can anyone ask God for it?"*

"Why do you ask, Jeff? Do you want to speak in tongues?"

"Yes," I replied.

"Okay. Go into the bathroom. I will come in there and pray and ask God to give you the gift of tongues."

So, I got up out of my chair and went into the bathroom. Moments later, Larry came in and, before he prayed over me, said, *"I want* **YOU** *to ask God for His gift of tongues."*

"Okay."

As he put his hands on and prayed over me, I asked God to let me have the gift of speaking in tongues. When he was finished, I asked, *"What now?"*

"You have to wait and see what happens," he said.

I then hugged him and told him I would see him later. I then walked back out to the reception area where James was waiting and said, *"Let's go."* As we walked out the door, he asked, *"What were you **laughing** at back there?"*

"You heard me?" I asked with surprise.

"Yes. Everyone heard you."

I told James that Larry told me a joke, and then **quickly** changed the subject. On our walk back to the house, I told James I was going to get a bite to eat for lunch while we were out.

I took my food back to the house, ate it, and went to lie down in my room. They had moved me yet again to another room *(for some reason, they make you change rooms a lot)*. My new spot was in a room at the front of the house. It was the largest room and had two sets of bunk beds. I shared the room with Mark and Bob. Fortunately, I still had the bottom bunk that was located next to a window. The top bunk was empty…for the moment. Honestly, I was really glad they moved me out of the room I shared with Dan.

As I was laying across my bed looking at the book the lady from the church gave me, Dave came into the room and asked me if I knew how to sheetrock and spackle. I looked at him and said, *"Yeah…why?"*

"I might have a job in South Jersey. A lady with a condominium needs some painting and spackling done. Do you want to help me out?"

"Okay," I said.

He paused and said, *"First, I need to see if you can spackle."*

I got up and went with him over to his friend's house. We walked into the living room where I could see water damage from a leak in his ceiling. I explained, *"I could fix it, but the next time it rains hard, you're going to see the ceiling start showing a yellow stain mark. Before I can fix the ceiling, you're going to need to fix your roof first – at least the area where the leak is coming into your living room."* It took me two days to fix the ceiling. After it dried, it was hard to see where the patch was that I made. Both men were impressed with the job I had done, and I knew that was one way I can get out of the house; by working.

See, if we did a job for someone, they would donate money to the program. Some would even ask if it was okay to put some money on our account (whoever did the job). Our "account" was an envelope management of the house kept in the office for us.

Since my arrival, I helped put some posts in the ground for a deck. I also framed out a floor in a garage and got hurt on that job when I hit my ring finger with a handheld sledgehammer while lining up the floor beams. It gave me a bad cut, but I didn't go to the hospital. I just wrapped it up and went back to the house. The next morning, it was throbbing like it had its own heartbeat. When I finally went to the hospital, it was too late for them to give me stitches.

The beginning of June, I worked a **lot**. Some of the people I helped out gave Dave money for me that he put in my envelope at the house. I even worked at the restaurant across from the church, vacuuming and washing dishes. Deacon Jones even talked to me about waiting tables and taking orders on Sundays after church. Life was, indeed, good!

CHAPTER TWENTY-FIVE
THE HEALING RUSH OF WIND

After a while, I stopped counting the days I had lived at the transitional house. It seemed like being able to work was helping me adjust. I loved working. I recall how hard it was for me to keep a job while I was using heroin. Before I knew it, getting heroin became my job. I used to get up early to go out on the block to see if I could find anyone out there that time of day. Sometimes, there would be someone available, but there were those days when I couldn't find anyone. As a result, I would either call out of work or go in late.

What really bothered me was that I was in my late 30s and living with my parents. I would be up and could hear my dad getting ready for work every morning. He had one or two more years before retirement. I was bothered because I couldn't understand how I allowed a drug to control my life like it did, to the point that I couldn't even keep a job for more than six months.

The morning that James left the program, the question was asked, *"Who gave him money to leave?"* I knew it wasn't me. I *suspected* he might have gotten the money from his brother.

Since I first arrived, I saw at least five men leave the program. I know that if I didn't have the threat of that drug charge hanging over me, I would've been gone, too. I know from experience that when the drug calls for you to come back to it, the struggle is real. That demon of addiction tries to kill you, and it won't let you go just because you want to quit. Long after the detox phase, it's still there riding your back because it's a part of what and who you are. No way can a simple detox get that demon off your back. The fight then becomes trying your hand at normalcy, even though you don't remember what normal is anymore for you. There are triggers all around — those things that make you constantly think about using again. Emotions and feelings are hard to understand, especially knowing you haven't dealt with anything for so long. Add on the need to be aware of every situation after years of saying **"F**K IT!"**, and the expectation that I live life on life's terms non-medicated is truly a battle for the ages!

Nonetheless, on this day I feel a little better. I was in a depressed state of mind after seeing people come and go through the program. Who's to say who will make it and who will relapse?

God, I am tired of being sick and tired! I'm tired of still not being able to stop using heroin! My biggest fear remained that God would lock me up for all those years. How crazy is it for me to know the consequences of my actions, yet I still want to find a way to get high? Am I sick, to the point that my life no longer holds meaning to me?

The church was making preparations for Holy Convocation. Men and women pastors would come to the church every night that week, and during the day, they would teach and preach from the Bible.

That week of Holy Convocation was beautiful. I never experienced anything like that before in church. The choir sounded great, and the pastors who came were awesome! I heard from God every night.

I will never forget the night of June 30, 2002. I heard from God so clearly. I would ask Him a question, and the answer would come from the preacher! At the end of the service, she asked for a sacrificial offering. I told God I didn't have any money that night but that I was going to get paid the next day, which was July 1st. The preacher then said, *"If you don't have it now, give it tomorrow."* See what I mean about the **immediate** response?

So, after the service, I went to the restaurant to work. Quite a few people from the service came there to eat. I saw Minister Boyd, so I went over to him and said, *"I want to give the rest of my money as an offering to the church – after I pay my rent."* He said, *"Okay. I will take care of it for you."* I thanked him and went back to work.

By the time we got home that night, it was after midnight. I was exhausted and went straight to bed.

At 3:00 a.m., I was awakened out of my sleep by a voice that spoke through my spirit. The voice said, *"I need you to come outside."* I lifted the blind, looked out the window, and said, *"It's still dark. You know I get up around 5:00 to have my coffee with*

You." I let the blind go, laid back down, and closed my eyes. Suddenly, I got sharp pains in my stomach. Shortly after, it started to bubble. I grabbed the air freshener off my dresser and went into the bathroom. As I finished up and while still seated, He spoke again to my spirit: **"I need you to come outside."** That time, there was a sense of urgency in His voice.

So, I went out the back door, and He asked me, *"Are you afraid?"*

"No," I replied.

"Come close to the edge." I took two steps forward and then felt a rush of wind come from the left of where I stood. All of a sudden, my body began to bend backward, to the point I started to hear my spine start to pop. I held my arms out as if He was going to pick me up and started crying, saying, **"Abba, Abba. Heal me, Father."** I bent so far back, I could feel my spine moving and cracking—but there was **NO** pain. I cried not because of any pain; rather, I was overwhelmed with **joy**! I laid prostrate on the porch and repeatedly said, *"Thank You, God."*

After that, He said, *"It is done."*

I then got up and went to my room. I was so excited, I grabbed my Bible and read from the Book of Jonah.

When the daylight finally dawned, I wondered if I dreamt the experience. What exactly happened to me? After morning prayer, I went into the back yard and stood close to the house. I needed to see how far I could bend backward without falling. I was pleasantly surprised at the result! I knew

I couldn't bend anywhere near as far as I did at that moment. I wondered if I should tell anyone about what happened, but decided against it. They might have thought I was crazy!

After that experience with God, I talked to Him **ALL** the time, just as I would a best friend. I could hear Him through His Word when I read the Bible **and** when I went to church.

CHAPTER TWENTY-SIX
VICIOUS AND THE PUP

God continued to show up and show out in my life.

One day, Joe was driving, and Paul sat up front with him. I sat in the second row, and Dan sat in the back. The van was parked in a parking lot across from the house, with the front facing a brick building. When Joe started the van, I saw him put his hand on the gear-shifter to move it. I then got a vision that instead of him shifting into reverse, he placed the gear in drive and we headed towards the wall. As his hand was still on the gear, I said to him, *"You have to put it in reverse."* As I spoke, the van crept toward the wall. Paul turned and looked at me in shock. **"How did you know he was in drive?"**

"God showed me," I said. I then fell silent and stared out the window. After that day, I was no longer afraid to ride with Joe. I guess I felt that God was indeed with me.

A couple of days later *(I recall it being a Friday)*, Minister Boyd was going to allow me to go to my parents' house to pick up some court papers. The night before I went home, I saw myself in a dream. I was in my parents' back yard and walking to the pen behind our garage where I had my dog, Vicious. As I was walking, a white and tan spotted dog came out of my parents' house toward me. I tried to grab it because I didn't want the dog to run away. Instead, it followed me to the pen where Vicious was…and then I woke up.

That day, I got up, had my coffee early with God, and read from my devotional before going to early prayer. When we returned to the house, I did my chores and then went to sit in the back yard while waiting for Minister Boyd to come so we could have our group session. I stayed in the back, lifting weights and talking with God. I had a lot of questions for Him, with one of them being, **"Why did You leave me out there so long in my addiction?"** My conversation with Him continued. *"I suffered so long out there. I cried out countless times to You while lying in my bed at home. The only voice I heard was the enemy's as he tried to destroy me. Why did I have to suffer for so long?"*

God let me know that He was preparing me for something greater in my life. What I went through wasn't just for me; I carried the weight and was weighed down with the afflictions of many.

Dan's voice broke through my thoughts. He came to the back door and said, *"Minister Boyd isn't here, and Dave is in the office on the phone. We are going to have our own group, so come on in. We're about to start."*

I went inside and sat around the table with the others. Mark said, *"Let's go around the room and let everyone share a scripture."* While the others took their turn, I asked God, *"What would You have me to share from Your Word?"* He gave me a passage from the Gospel of Matthew 6:33:

"But seek ye first the kingdom of God, and His righteousness, and all these things shall be added unto you."

I then shared with the group what the Spirit said to me about that passage. *"To me, that means this: Find God in your life so that you can find out why He created you and what purpose He has for you to do for Him. And while you are seeking Him, you will see the hurt and pain you inflicted while living in sin, but it is the love that He gives you that causes you to want to live a righteous life with Him while here on Earth. Today, I have peace in my life. I feel good about where I am today. I may not be where I want to be, but I am definitely glad that I am not where I used to be!"* I ended with that and then thanked God for allowing me to share.

After we finished our impromptu group session, Dave came into the kitchen and said, *"I heard the group. It sounded like some of y'all were listening!"* We laughed and then he began delegating our duties for the day.

I approached Dave and asked him what time I would be able to pick up the court papers at my parents' house.

"You can go now," he said. *"I need to use the van after you get back to pick up some doughnuts for this weekend. We have to take the seats out of the van first."*

Every time we went to pick up the doughnuts, we had to remove the seats to make room for the load. I suppose that's a write-off for the company that donates them. We had to sell them right away before they went bad. We kept them next door in the Mercy House, which used to be where the program was run from, but there was a fire in that house before I entered the program, so they switched and made the Mercy House the transitional facility.

So, after Dave finished telling us the schedule for the day and the seats had been removed from the van, Dan and I left to go to my parents' house. Along the way, we talked about the people who left the program and how, when the Summer comes, people would rather be on the streets than in a program. I also mentioned that James told me he was going to ask if he could go home, but he chose to get up early one morning and just left—and then returned two days later.

Dan said, *"You know, he even asked me to borrow some money, but I told him no. I didn't want to be the one who helped him leave."* I nodded my head in agreement, as I knew that conversation well. He then asked, *"Do you know where he got the money from?"*

"No," I replied, although I had my suspicions.

"I think his brother gave it to him. Wow! I would have put both of them out of the program," Dan said softly.

Soon, we arrived at my parents' house. As we pulled up, I saw my father on the porch drinking his coffee. I told Dan I wouldn't be long and hopped out of the van. I walked up the driveway toward the house and said hi to my dad.

"What are you doing here, Jeff? Please tell me you didn't leave the program," he said with obvious concern.

"Do you see any bags, dad? I like where I am. I now have a relationship with God."

He smiled and said, "I am glad you have come to know God for yourself. So, what brings you home today?"

"Mom said she has a letter from the courts for me. Did you see it?" I flipped through where we kept the mail and couldn't locate the letter.

"Go check with your mother. She's upstairs. She might have it in our room."

I went upstairs and, as soon as my mom saw me, she asked, **"What are you doing here?"**

"Oh, no. You, too? What? You and dad aren't happy to see me? He asked me the same thing! I just came to get that letter from the courts." I then heard a dog bark. The sound came from my younger brother's room. I asked about what kind of dog he had.

"A puppy," my mom responded.

I remembered the dream. "Is that puppy white with tan spots on it?"

"Yeah! **How did you know that?**"

I immediately walked out of her room and went to my brother's room. When I opened the door, the puppy looked exactly as I saw her in my dream. Just like in my dream, she even followed me outside when I went to see my dog, Vicious.

It was as if I was living the dream I had the night before. **That freaked me out!**

After I played with Vicious and put the puppy back in my brother's room, I went and kissed my mom goodbye. As she handed me the letter, she asked, *"What's the matter with you, Jeffrey?"*

I told her that God showed me a dream last night and about everything from the time I first saw the puppy. *"It was like déjà vu, mom!"*

"Maybe God is calling you for something, son."

*"I know, mom. But why **me**?"*

"You should be asking God that question," she stated, as a knowing smile spread across her face.

I said my goodbyes to my parents, and Dan and I headed back to the program. When we returned, Paul, Mark, and Joe were getting donations for the doughnuts. As I started to walk inside, I looked over at the guys and considered going to help them out. God, however, wanted me to read in my room. So, I went upstairs and got settled in. I started to feel as if God was separating me from the rest of the guys in the house.

Once settled, I asked God, *"What is it that You want me to read?"* He led me to the Book of 1st Samuel 17, where David kills the giant, Goliath. As I was reading, I imagined a giant in my life—one who needed its head cut off, too. It wasn't long before I knew God was talking directly to me about my swearwords.

I came to the program swearing, and although I've tried to stop, my vocabulary was limited. I substituted by using words of profanity, as it was the way I talked for years. I recognized that as one of my "character defects," which was a product of my drug habit. As I continued reading, I found a verse that spoke to that defect and would take off the head of swearwords from me:

"This day will the LORD deliver thee into mine hand, and I will smite thee, and take thine head from thee; and I will give the carcasses of the host of the Philistines this day unto the fowls of the air, and to the wild beasts of the Earth, that all the Earth may know that there is a God in Israel."
~ 1st Samuel 17:46 ~

CHAPTER TWENTY-SEVEN
TRUSTING AND BELIEVING

Thank You, Jesus, for 135 days clean! The date was Saturday, July 20th. I knew in my heart that it was God who directed me to the program. When I accepted Jesus as my Lord and Savior on March 7, 2002, my life changed for the better. I never knew how much I needed Him in my life. I now know that I am alive because of Jesus. God gave me a second chance at life!

Deacon Mark brought a visitor with him to morning prayer. We started off by saying our prayers and giving thanks for what God had done in our life that day. Deacon then introduced the visitor and told us he was going to share his testimony with us.

As the visitor was speaking, I realized he had a remarkable testimony. He spoke of an encounter he had with God. I then asked of God, *"If what happened to me on the back porch was also an experience with You, God, show me a sign."* At the time, we were sitting in a circle in the room where the children and elderly would sit during services. I was seated to the right of the visitor. He then looked directly at me and said, **"Trust and believe."**

I knew then that God was speaking to me about trusting Him.

God, I know there is something You are calling me to do. I hear You in my spirit talking with me. When I ask You a question, You are always there to answer. God, I want to do whatever it is that You are preparing me for. I know I've had doubts about what You did to and for me. I was afraid to say anything to anyone, but I do believe You are real. I want to have an intimate relationship with You.

"He that dwelleth in the secret place of the Most High shall abide under the shadow of the Almighty."
~ Psalms 91:1 ~

Jeffrey G. Mitchell, Sr.

CHAPTER TWENTY-EIGHT
HE WAS ALWAYS THERE FOR ME

I entered the program without a clue that Jesus is the Son of God. I never knew I could have a one-on-one relationship with Him. He has shown me visions and dreams. Christ is alive and seated at the right hand of God, making intercession on our behalf. I've never seen Him, but I believe in the very depths of my heart that **HE LIVES**. As my relationship with Him grows, He is working on my character defects. I truly believe that what I went through in life was to bring me to the transitional house where I could find God for myself.

I recall leaving my parents' home one day to buy some heroin. As I walked down the driveway, I thought about the many years of my life that my addiction stole from me and how my life had changed for the worst. I saw no hope or future. However, by the time I approached the end of the hill in the park, a feeling of my addiction coming to an end overcame me. At the time, I didn't know why I had that feeling, but I now know today that God was there with me, even during the darkest days of my life.

At my lowest point, I was locked up in jail. I couldn't catch my breath because of an asthma attack. I fell to my knees and called on God saying, *"I have had enough. If You don't help me now, let me die!"* I then got up, wet some tissues, and wrote the word **'HELP'** on the wall of my cell that faced the camera. An officer came back to where they were holding me and said, ***"Take that down."*** After I took it down, I told him I was having an asthma attack and needed my inhaler.

I cried out to God in my affliction and wondered why He left me alone when I needed Him the most. Today, I think back and thank God for being there when I thought I was all alone and that no one cared for me.

CHAPTER TWENTY-NINE
IT'S NOT MY BIRTHDAY!

One time, the guys and I attended a Youth Conference in Asbury Park. I noticed the church was kind of small, but it was nice. We found some seats, but as the service progressed, someone asked the older people to move to the balcony so that the youth could be downstairs for the service. Once the children were downstairs, a woman came out to speak. She told us she was called to ministry at the age of fifteen.

During this time, a lady came and sat next to me. At first, I thought nothing of her sudden presence—until she started worshiping God as tears streamed down her face. She was in full worship, as was I. The service was amazing! The woman sitting next to me touched my arm, so I turned towards her. With tears in her eyes, she said, *"God wants me to tell you that you have just been delivered."* I instantly got happy, and she got happy for me. We both shouted, **"GLORY! GLORY TO GOD! HALLELUJAH! HALLELUJAH!"** I then hugged her and said, *"Thank you."* I was overjoyed to hear God had delivered me!

To think: I thought that because it was a *Youth Conference*, I wouldn't get anything out of it. Well, lesson learned. I will never think like **THAT** again.

The next day, I told Minister Boyd about the experience, but he was concerned about who it was who told me about my deliverance. *"Did you know her?"* he asked.

"No."

"Have you seen her before?"

Again, I said, *"No."*

His concern was genuine and justified. I learned that everyone in the church isn't there looking for God. Some have their own twisted agenda for being there. I also heard about some of the women taking advantage of men who were in a program, finding us weak and easy to manipulate. I knew Minister Boyd asked me those questions out of concern, but I also knew it was God who placed that woman next to me. It seemed as if He moved people around during that service until she was next to me, just so He could use her to relay His message.

I believed I had been delivered…but from **what**? I was so messed up from my addiction and other flaws. Nonetheless, I chose to walk in my deliverance and wait to see God's glory in my life. Plus, I had already thanked Him!

"Now faith is the substance of things hoped for,
the evidence of things not seen."
~ Hebrews 11:1 ~

Later that day, Dan came into my room and gave me a portable cassette player, along with the earpiece that went along with it. I asked, *"What is this? An early birthday present? You know my birthday is August 2nd, man!"*

"No," he said. *"My mom just sent me a new one, so I thought maybe you'd like this one."* I accepted the gift and thanked him. *"Do you need some tapes, too?"*

"Yes."

"Okay. I will let you listen to a couple of mine until you get some of your own."

I noticed the batteries were getting weak in the cassette player, so I got up and went next door to the Mercy House. I remembered seeing some batteries there when we were cleaning up one day. I went straight to the living room area and opened the dresser drawer. Inside, there was a remote control to a TV. I opened the back, and there was a set of batteries still inside. I removed them and then saw that there were a few cassette tapes in the drawer, too. I looked through them and read what was written on each. I grabbed three of them and a new pack of batteries, and then returned to my room.

Once back in my room, I put one of the tapes into the player. The tape was titled "Dry Bones." It was recorded on September 21, 1990, during a Men's Only Night Service. That was 12 years ago! I wondered why the recording was still in the drawer. As I listened, I could tell it was Bishop speaking. He spoke out of the Book of Ezekiel, the 37th chapter. I was in tune with what he was saying and imagined him speaking directly to me and all that I had been through in the past. I was amid my addiction when he preached that sermon—and I do mean **PREACH!**

God, is this the place You had for me to come? Why did You want me to find this tape? I don't really understand, but I know this tape is for me. It was left behind so that I could have it.

I feel God is controlling my life. I see things differently, and my heart is not as cold. I wish everyone would accept Jesus as their Lord and Savior and have an intimate relationship with God. For so long, I was estranged from a relationship with God, but Jesus made it possible for me to know the Father once again. You see, I have always believed in God, but my sins kept me separated from Him. I am now born again! I am not going to say I am perfect—after all, **NO ONE IS**—but I am willing to make changes in my life, especially now that I have been given a second chance to learn how to live a righteous life for God.

"And I will raise Me up a faithful priest that shall do according to that which is in Mine heart and in My mind, and I will build him a sure house; and he shall walk before Mine anointed forever."
~ 1st Samuel 2:35 ~

Jeffrey G. Mitchell, Sr.

CHAPTER THIRTY
IT'S MY BIRTHDAY!

The date was August 2nd — my birthday. I did not spend my day at the transitional house because the counselor from the Stepping Out of Darkness meeting came and took Mark and me to his mother's house the day before. Brian was preparing for their annual picnic in Rahway Park, so we spent the night helping load up the van with chairs, tables, and deep fryers for frying turkeys. While they were preparing all of the food at his mom's house, Mark and I were in his mother's basement playing pool and watching TV.

The next day at the park, other people from different programs were there as well. I was happy to spend my birthday at a picnic. I was also able to let my mother know about it, and she and my godmother came, along with my oldest sister. By the time they arrived, I was playing a game of volleyball. When I saw them, I walked over to the car and climbed in with them. I was surprised to see my big sister. She asked me how I was doing and how I felt. I told her that the grace of God saved me and I have a relationship with Him. I then asked them if they wanted me to fix them each a plate of food because they didn't want to get out of the car. My sister and I made my mom and godmother a plate and went back to the car. While they were eating, I sat in the car with them, and we talked. I told them I was going to register with the Union County College in Elizabeth to get my GED in the Fall, and that I had already spoken with Minister Boyd about my plans, to which he said, *"GREAT!"* After they left, I went over to the pond where the paddleboats were and enjoyed the rest of my day.

Once the event was over, the guys and I helped pack up and took Brian's things back to his mother's house. After we unloaded the rental truck, he drove us back to the house.

I know it was because of God and His favor that I was able to celebrate my birthday in a fun way that year.

CHAPTER THIRTY-ONE
AN UNFAMILIAR SHIFT IN THE ATMOSPHERE

"I am the True Vine, and my Father is the Husbandman. Every branch in Me that bears not fruit, He taketh away; and every branch that bears fruit, He prunes it, that it may bring forth more fruit."
~ John 15:1-2 ~

One day, while Minister Boyd was having group, Bob just got up out of his seat and announced he was leaving the program. I wasn't surprised that he wanted to leave. It was just a matter of time. He only had a couple of months to do, so I went upstairs to see if I could get him to change his mind. As I spoke, he was steady grabbing his clothes out of his drawers and closet. Dan then said, *"If he wants to leave, let him."* That didn't stop me from trying to convince him that he needed to stay and complete the program. Regardless of what I said, he was adamant about leaving. Nothing I said was getting through to him. That spirit of addiction was calling him back, coupled with the fact that he was still getting high while in the house.

Not long after Bob's departure, the program as a whole made a major shift. Joe and Anthony completed the program — and Dan walked out of it. We then got two new people, but it wasn't the same for me. Everyone I was familiar with had left.

Lord, may I serve You, for You're the vine that nourishes the fruit that clings to the branches of faith, which brings forth the fruit of the vine, whose miracles shall be seen in trials and tribulations, which brings forth the fruit of righteousness in God. You're the sun that gives life and strength. You're also the shade that covers and shields, for I rest in You, yielding righteous fruit in due season.

I wanted nothing more than to complete the program. Up until that point in my life, I hadn't completed many things in my life. I would always start with good intentions on finishing, but would fall short before achieving anything. I saw those who were able to complete the program. I also watched those who left for their own reasons. There were also those who stayed a day or two before deciding the program was not for them. Were there **ANY** guarantees in life? Some will make it, while others are **doomed** to have to do it all over again. I am saddened for those who left on their own, but as for me, I still had a chance to reach completion. Still, I was afraid of failing again.

I am calling on you, God. All that I have known through my life here on Earth will not get me through this program. I know not to trust my judgment. My life was full of confusion when I came here. Since that time, I have accepted Jesus and my life has changed for the better. God, you brought me this far. Please don't leave me to depend on my own understanding.

My life had changed dramatically since I arrived at the transitional house, but I wasn't the only one who noticed. There was a woman who sat a couple of rows behind me in church who appeared to be watching me. One day, she came over to the restaurant to eat after service. I was her waiter on this occasion *(I had been taking orders there for about a week before this encounter)*. Roughly two weeks passed after that, and I didn't see her in church.

One Sunday, I was in church and service was just beginning. A man stood up and began sharing his testimony. Suddenly, I could no longer hear what he was saying. I saw his mouth moving, but in my spirit, I heard something completely different than what he verbalized.

That day, the woman from the restaurant sat two rows in front of me. She was with another lady who kept urging her to sit next to me. The woman kept telling her no. Both would then turn to look at me, and I would smile at them. Then, I heard from the man who was giving his testimony, *"Does he know what's going on?"* Next thing I knew, a different lady in the row in front of me turned and looked at me. I smiled at her, too. She said, *"Yes, he knows what's going on."*

I was in a **spiritual** realm hearing **everything** being said, all while the regular church service was going on around me.

I believe the enemy wanted to check up on me to see how I was doing and what was going on with me. For whatever the reason, none of the women would get close to or sit next to me. The two women finally got up and left the service as soon as the choir started to worship the Lord in song. After that day, I never saw either of them in the church again.

Why would God let me know that the enemy was interested in how I was doing in the program?

Once back at the house and in the quiet of my room, I had another conversation with God. *"God, what are You trying to tell me? I heard every word that was said in a spiritual realm while church service was going on. How is it that they could just come and see how I am doing here?"*

He replied, *"I wanted you to see just how close the enemy truly is to you. When Allen asked you to borrow some money, that planted a thought of using heroin again, which consumed you while you were in the New Beginnings meeting. You were overwhelmed by that suggestion, and your thoughts were consumed with a spiritual war that night. However, when you told Dan what was going on with you and he shared My Word with you, that made the spirit of addiction flee from you that night. Then, when you walked with Bob on that supposed dentist visit, that same spirit was on Allen, which transferred to Bob. I am with you, my son; but the enemy has known you and is interested in keeping you. He will visit from time to time to see if he can get you back — and he won't always show up in the same spirit. Take heed to My Word, son, for you shall find life."*

> *"When the unclean spirit is gone out of a man, he walked through dry places, seeking rest, and finding none. Then he said, 'I will return into my house from whence I came out'; and when he is come, he findeth it empty, swept, and garnished. Then get him, and taketh with himself seven other spirits more wicked than himself, and they enter in and dwell there: and the last state of that man is worse than the first. Even so, shall it be also unto this wicked generation."*
> **~ Matthew 12:43-45 ~**

God continued to speak: *"That spirit of addiction is not about to let you live your life now, especially after being with you so long. He is restless and agitated because he no longer dwells in you. Now, he has to have his day of reckoning and be held accountable for what happened because he was so close in manipulating you to believe that your life was no longer worth living as an addict.*

"How many times did you try to stop using drugs while in your addiction? How many times did you go through detoxes and 28-day programs? Why would you always find yourself drawn back to what was familiar to you? What was the driving force that brought you back to the grips of death?

"There was a lingering shadow that was determined to have you, all while making you feel miserable about yourself. That spirit also manipulated you into believing that heroin can make you feel better. That is how it kept you so that death wouldn't seem so bad whenever he came to visit you."

CHAPTER THIRTY-TWO
THE BEE AND THE SPIDER

I'm buzzing along minding my own business when I see some honey in a tree. As I glanced while passing by, I noticed a spider looking at me! The lure of honey was enticing me. Now, caught in a web...buzzing, buzzing, buzzing...trying to get free, while the spider is gazing and thinking, *"Hmm... My next meal it will be!"*

The spider climbed down her web. With quickness, she spun another web, trying to entangle me. I continued to buzz, buzz, buzz, trying to get free. The more I buzzed, the more entangled I grew to be.

As she got close to me, I stopped buzzing and the web loosened. When that spider came to bite, my stinger set me free. Now, the other spiders around that tree began to wonder how that bee got that spider up in his honey tree?

"And we know that all things work together for good to them that love God, to them who are called according to His purpose."
~ **Romans 8:28** ~

CHAPTER THIRTY-THREE
SMARTER AND BETTER

Twenty years ago was the last time I set foot inside of a school. On that day, Mark and I rode the train to Elizabeth to make my re-entry into the land of academia. I was excited about being in school again, knowing that it would be different for me. I wasn't looking for acceptance or trying to find where I might fit in. Rather, I wanted to **LEARN**—and get my GED.

It felt good to be out of the house and going to school again. I sat in front of the class and paid attention to what the teacher said.

(The funny thing is this: I could have done the same thing the first time around, but I was a follower, trying to fit in with a group of people who, just like me, were looking for their identity. It was much like the blind leading the blind.)

I chose to reenter school to better myself. I may not have been the smartest person in the class, but I was the one who wanted to learn. Even my homework assignments were completed. I was grateful for the second chance and intended to make the most of it.

Back when I was in high school and had the chance to learn to obtain my diploma, I didn't think it was *that* important at the time. As such, academics took a backseat to my self-assigned priorities, which I now see got me nowhere in life. I did not utilize the free education that was afforded me at the expense of so many who sacrificed themselves for the opportunity. It sometimes saddens me to know I threw away my youth on drugs and alcohol while in school.

Jeffrey G. Mitchell, Sr.

CHAPTER THIRTY-FOUR
197 DAYS CLEAN! BUT WHO'S COUNTING?

Back at the house, there were only six of us left. It appeared that after the last two came, they were not allowing anyone else into the program. There was a rumor going around that we were to be the last class to graduate from the program, but it was just a rumor for the moment. Some of the guys let it bother them, asking questions like, *"If they close the doors to the program, where would we go from here?"*

As for me, I continued working on some of my character defects. Apparently, some of the men thought I whined when I spoke. Dave also pointed it out to me, so who better to ask about it than God? Like always, He didn't keep me waiting for a response. God let me know what **HE** wanted me to work on.

One night, I was at the back door on the second floor. I had to take the garbage out that night. So, me being me, I was going to toss it down into the cans in the back yard. Well, of course, I missed and still had to go down to pick up all the garbage that fell out of the bags. Why didn't I just go down and put it in the can in the first place? By the time I made it down to the cans, I had realized: **WOW! I DO WHINE!** I had to laugh at myself. I actually sounded like James! He used to whine just like that when he talked.

Once aware that I did, indeed, whine sometimes when I talked, I needed to see how to change it—**with God's help**. It appeared He took my profanity away, as I stopped using that foul language!

My journey through school continued. At this point, it had been roughly two weeks, and I was truly enjoying myself. I would participate in morning prayer with the group, and then Mark and I would catch the train to school. I couldn't fail to notice that we were given new opportunities to practice being independent. We were allowed to make some decisions on our own as well. I was glad that the Lord was directing me and believe my steps were being ordered by Him.

One night, I counted my calendar days clean. **197 DAYS!** That meant a whole lot to me, as I recalled the times I couldn't stay clean for more than twenty-one days. I know that my sobriety is not my doing. I felt so good about where I was in life:

- In school working towards getting my GED.
- Willingly participated in meetings **AND** enjoyed them.
- No longer used any type of mind-altering chemicals just to "feel good" about myself.
- I loved going to church.
- Most of all, I had an intimate relationship with God, and it was that relationship with the Father that kept me.

Jeffrey G. Mitchell, Sr.

My biggest fear was that I would wake up in a hospital and be told I was in a coma. Upon awakening, I would be told that my new lifestyle was just a dream.

With my life being as sweet as it was, it was sometimes challenging to come to grips with what's been going on in my life. When I cried at night, they were tears of joy and sorrow: happy for where I was at the age of 41; sorrowful because I didn't understand why God left me out there for so long. I had become a walking coma patient for quite some time while in my addition; aware of my surroundings, yet feeling nothing.

CHAPTER THIRTY-FIVE
I UNDERSTOOD JONAH

The date was September 21st. My body was **so** tired. I wanted to rest, but I also needed to have my time with God that morning. I climbed out of bed, went into the kitchen, and turned the tea kettle on so that I could make my cup of coffee. While waiting for the water to come to a boil, I went into the bathroom to wash up and prepare for 7:00 a.m. early prayer. I thought to myself, *"I love being up by myself early in the mornings,"* as I made my way to the back porch, coffee in hand.

I then spoke to God about the program ending. *"God, I don't know what's going to happen to me. I was supposed to do at least 13 months in a program for drug court. The transitional house told me this is a 13-month program. Why is it that now, when I want to actually finish a program, they suddenly pick* **THIS** *year to end it? That doesn't seem fair to me. I am scared about leaving this place. No one has told us how much longer we will even be here or what they intend to do with us who want to maintain our sobriety. God, I am really started to feel scared about going back home. I like where I am. There's a feeling of security here for me. What do I do if drug court says I have to do my last four months in another program? Please, God: I need Your help. Should I tell Minister Boyd what happened to me? Maybe then, they might keep the program."*

As I finished my coffee and time alone with God, I could hear the rest of the guys getting up. I went to lie across my bed for a few minutes until it was time to leave for prayer. I reflected on when I first entered the program and how I didn't want to be there. As life would have it, I grew to like being there, especially because so many people were very kind to me.

After prayer and our chores, I went into the back yard to lift weights, only because we had nothing on the schedule about any work that needed to be done. When I thought about it, we had been doing less and less work for others, but I still went to the restaurant after church to help out there.

While working out my muscles and looking up at the sky, I thought about the Book of Jonah. I then got up, went to my room, and grabbed my Bible. I turned to and read Jonah 2:1-2:

"Then Jonah prayed unto the LORD God out of the fish's belly. And said, 'I cried by reason of mine affliction unto the LORD, and He heard me; out of the belly of hell cried I, and Thou heard my voice.'"

It was then I learned that because God allowed me to fall off that ladder, I began to seek God and cry out to Him while asking, *"Why did You let me fall?"* Although He never said *why*, a host of other questions came from that experience, prompting me to ask and seek His guidance on many things. It seemed like He quickened me to know Him.

I believe God already knew I wasn't going to remain in the program for the entire 13 months, as it was His way for me to establish my relationship with Him. I definitely had no idea about how to have a relationship with Him before entering the transitional house. I liken myself to Jonah, in that because Jonah didn't accept the call on his life and do what God wanted him to do *(go to the city of Nineveh and speak to them about their wickedness)*, God had to do **SOMETHING** to get his attention.

So, God, why are You showing **me** all of these things? Who am I that You would want to use me? My God, if it is Your plan to use me, make it known unto me. Show me that which You would have me to do for You. I am Thy servant, LORD. I wish to serve as an empty vessel. Fill me with Your heart's desires and speak **clearly** to me so that I will make few mistakes.

CHAPTER THIRTY-SIX
ONE WORD: BLESSED

"The hand of the LORD was upon me, and carried me out in the Spirit of the LORD, and set me down in the midst of the valley, which was full of bones."
~ Ezekiel 37:1 ~

I knew the tape I found called "Dry Bones" was just for me. I listened to that recording over and over, hoping to receive some kind of understanding about what God was saying.

The revelation was amazing!

I was the dry bones that He spoke about. When I entered the program, I did not have the breath of God in me; neither was I able to hear His Word to permit sinew to come upon me. God put His breath in me and made me hope again. I found a reason to live! HE placed me upon my feet again on solid ground. **My God, my God! Am I a testimony?**

"My son, have no fear, for you have found Me. When you leave this place, I will be with you always. My Spirit have I placed in you to help direct your path."

I started to feel like a flower about to bloom, early in its season, while the dew of the morning moistened me. By a meadow, where a river runs near, in me were the memories of a seed, hurdling to and fro, carried upon the wind until it found just the right place for me. I still carried my dreams of a seed in the Earth; how I struggled as my roots were being drawn down, while my main body was rising above the ground and my roots were seeking their place in the soil.

Time seemed to be flying by, with me working on Sundays after church and attending school all week. I enjoyed the chill in the morning air, as the Fall season approached. My thoughts turned to leaving the program soon. I was aware that the place I was to return to had not changed — but I had. That in itself would be what made the difference when I went back home.

When I thought all was going well for me, I awoke early one Saturday, glanced at the clock, and said to myself, *"I'll get up in 15 minutes."* The next thing I saw was a horrible beast, **devouring** people. Body parts were laying in the snow with blood all around me. When the creature stood over me, I fell to the ground and curled up in a fetal position, knowing he was about to grab me. I then saw one word written over me:

BLESSED.

I then woke up, grabbed my clothes, and **RAN** to the church. When I got there, I asked God, *"Why did You show me **THAT**?"*

He explained: *"I want you to write what I showed you, and then you need to share this. A man watched a beast devour other people and then saw the beast coming towards him. As the beast towered over him, he fell to the ground and curled up in a fetal position. The only thing he then saw was the word* **"BLESSED"** *written over his head. It was then he realized the beast did not devour him.*

"The man then went to the Elders of the church to tell them what happened. They told him he needed to tell others. The next day, the man shared in prayer outside the church while holding hands with others, saying, **"BLESSED are we who are saved!"** *He then read from Psalms 44:7-8:*

"But you have saved us from our enemies and have put to shame those who hated us. In God, we boast all the day long and praise Your name forever."

"As the people praised Me, the sun rose over the buildings and people walked by looking at them saying, **'BLESSED are they who are saved!'"**

I was given that vision to share with **YOU** what God has done for me. Surely, He snatched me out of a life of hell. Me telling others about His mercy is all He is asking me to do for Him. I have **NO** problem sharing the Good News of Christ and what He has done for me!

CHAPTER THIRTY-SEVEN
HOME, SWEET HOME

On December 24, 2002, I was on my way home. My time at the transitional house ended on Christmas Eve. I am grateful that I gave my life to Christ and have a relationship with God. He gave me the Spirit of Truth, which will abide with me forever.

On Christmas Day, I was both nervous and happy to be home. I had a good night's rest, even though I had to camp out in the TV room. I no longer had a bedroom to call my own, so the TV room was converted into my temporary humble abode. What was more important was that I was home and happy to be there. I knew that everything else would work out for me in time.

One thing that was predominantly on my mind was going to meetings. I knew that Brian held his meetings on Saturdays just around the corner from my parents' house, so I would definitely go there. The entire time I was in the program, they wouldn't let us attend meetings like NA or AA. So, after the holidays, I wanted to go to a meeting—the first one since coming back home. I prayed and asked God what I should do.

That night, I walked to a meeting that was about 40 minutes away on the East end of town *(I lived on the West end)*.

Shortly before my arrival, God said to me, *"I want you to count how many times you hear them use swearwords* **AND** *how many times they say* **My** *name."* I figured I had no problem there! I could probably count both on my fingers.

I finally reached the place where they were having the NA meeting. Of course, I knew a lot of the faces that were there. I arrived a few minutes early, so I spent some time speaking to a couple of people before the meeting started. The first thing I remembered was that I had been delivered from heroin addiction and learned that life and death are in the power of the tongue—meaning when the people in the group started to introduce themselves, they would be inclined to say something like, *"My name is Andrew, and I am a heroin addict."*

I needed to hear from God **IMMEDIATELY**. I knew I was not supposed to attach negative things to me like that. He said to me, **"You say, 'My name is Jeff, and I have been delivered from using heroin.'"** So, when it was my turn to speak, I said, *"Hi. My name is Jeff. I have ten months of clean time and have been delivered from heroin."*

As the meeting continued, I heard different people share about their job or family or even just how they were feeling. Some would vent their frustrations.

I did as I was told and started counting on my fingers every time I heard a swearword. I would keep count in my head of every time I heard "God." I will tell you this: It wasn't long before I couldn't keep up with them using swearwords! **THAT** was likely a large part of the reason we were **prohibited** from participating in those types of meetings.

More than that, I understood why **GOD** didn't want me there. He did, after all, remove swearwords from my vocabulary. For me to sit around those who swore all the time, that spirit just might have tried to come back on me.

As such, I had **no** problem staying away from those meetings. They were not for me at all. My foundation was reading the Bible, going to church, and attending Bible Study classes. To walk in my deliverance, I needed to do those things with consistency.

CHAPTER THIRTY-EIGHT
FAMILIAR TERRITORY

Once home for good, my journey with God was just beginning. He was my guide in life and, through the reading of His Word, I found myself reassured that I was on the right path.

> *"Thy Word is a lamp unto my feet, and a light unto my path."*
> **~ Psalms 119:105 ~**

I knew who and what kept me. I also knew I had to continue walking with God, especially being home in "familiar" territory. I had to be diligent in finding out what God had for me. I was given a second chance at life, after my decision-making in the past only served to get me into trouble. The people around me hadn't changed, but the Word of God transformed me. To them, they might have still seen the "old me," but I knew that following God, they would no longer see the person I used to be. I was a new creature in Christ. The Word of God told me so! That was the reason why I read His Word: to stay on the path of righteousness. Should I have strayed for any reason, I was assured that the Word of God would lead and guide me back to Christ.

Still, I also needed a daily word to speak encouragement into my life while living and walking through the same town. I was among that number of those who had lost many battles. I also knew that many people were hesitant to return to the place where they had been beaten down so severely by their addiction, and often wanted to stay close to their support groups.

Things were different for me, though. When I walked through the same town, I knew where the battlefields were and recall how bad it was for me while in my addiction. It was comforting to walk with a word in my heart and the strength and might of the inner man in me as I trudged my way right through the minefields intended to take me **OUT**. I had a song in my heart and a battle cry of victory on my lips.

Sadly, many are still afflicted and spiritually wounded while battling the addiction beast.

"My son, give Me thine heart, and let thine eyes observe My ways."
~ **Proverbs 23:26** ~

~~~~~~~~~~

GOD SPEAKS:

"Many are called, and all can be redeemed, but only a few wish to do that which I have called them to do. Think of how this world would be if all My sons would take the time to connect with Me. I would take them on a journey and show them who they could be, if only they would take the time to hear from Me.

"Allow Me to come into your heart to take away the pain from years of separation from Me, so that you may see and observe My ways and learn what it means to be called "a son of Mine." My Son is in

me, and I am in My Son. What a joyful feeling it would be! But first, you must allow Me into your heart so that you can journey with Me. I only come to those who invite Me in. With free will, you must ask for Me.

"I will then show you a love you've never seen. I need you to choose Me, for I have already chosen you. Come. Allow Me to shape you in My hands, to mold you from My breath, and comfort you while you rest on My chest. I will protect you in My arms and love you from My heart, so you will know that you are My son, and I am Your God.

"'Abba' is what I hear when you call, and 'Well done, son,' is how I answered for you heard My call."

CHAPTER THIRTY-NINE
THE GIFT OF TONGUES

I was on the floor and had laid hands on myself. I started praying and was led to ask God in prayer for His gift of tongues. While still on the floor, I started speaking in tongues. I was surprised! I vaguely recall my daughter standing over me asking, *"Dad, are you okay?"* She then called my godmother because she didn't understand what was happening to me. I spoke in tongues for at least 20 minutes and after, went into a praise session to God.

I then got up, dressed, and went to sit on the front porch. It started again! I had no control over what was going on. Then, I walked to the park. As I walked, I spoke in tongues all the way. I looked up towards the sky, feeling guided by God, and continued to walk and speak in tongues. When I got close to my home, God said, *"Tell no one about what happened."*

That next Sunday in church, the Bishop said to the congregation, *"Those who want sanctification, line up on this side* [pointing to his right]. *All those who want to speak in tongues, come on this side* [pointing to his left]." As I rose out of my seat, I said to myself, *"I already speak in tongues, so let me go line up on the sanctification side."* As I neared the line, the Spirit instructed me to line up on the speaking in tongues side, so I did.

Bishop then prayed over all of us, and I started speaking in tongues in the church that day while he prayed. Later that night, I asked God, *"Why did You want me on the speaking in tongues side when You have already given me that gift?"*

He replied, *"Because I placed you under the Bishop, and you need to know that I am a God of order. You have been placed under his covering by Me."*

I must be honest here: Sometimes, God does **a lot** that makes no sense to me, but I keep on going, hoping that it will all make sense to me one day.

I recall the day I was walking my dog in the park and, as I walked up the hill by the backside of the school, I started speaking in tongues. That time, my hands were moving uncontrollably. I wasn't concerned, though. I was enjoying the newness of it all, although I didn't understand why it happened.

Another time, after I finished closing up the restaurant in my hometown, I walked home. Just like all the other times, I talked to God on my way *(He kept me company)*. As I entered the park from the West end entrance, I noticed how beautiful the moon was that night, so I walked across the grass near the brook that faced North. I could feel in my spirit I was about to speak in tongues. I said aloud, *"Sing in tongues, Abba."* I kid you not: **I sang in tongues!** I was overjoyed to be used by God! I then asked Him to give me the gift of interpretation of tongues. At least I could then know what was being said.

Turned By Grace

Well, that gift has not manifested in my life at the time of this writing, but I know one day it will. Until it does, I'm going to be happy with the gifts God **has** given me!

CHAPTER FORTY
THE NAMES OF GOD

One night, I was on my way to Bible Study at the middle school on 8th Street—the same place where Sunday services were held. I wanted to know the different names of God. I talked to Him about it earlier that day. While we sat in the cafeteria waiting on whoever was going to teach that night, I sat across from a friend of my godmother. We talked for a while and then she handed me a piece of paper with the different names of God written on it. I smiled at her and said, *"That was one of the things I asked God for today."*

She laughed and said, *"He **IS** an awesome God!"*

So, I looked down at the paper, and it had **ALL** of the names and their meanings:

- **JEHOVAH-TSIDKENU**
  - "Jehovah our Righteousness"
- **JEHOVAH-M'KADDESH**
  - "Jehovah who sanctifies"
- **JEHOVAH-SHALOM**
  - "Jehovah is Peace"
- **JEHOVAH-SHAMAH**
  - "Jehovah is there"
- **JEHOVAH-ROPHE**
  - "Jehovah heals"

- **JEHOVAH-JIREH**
  - "Jehovah's provision shall be seen"
- **JEHOVAH-NISSI**
  - "Jehovah my Banner"
- **JEHOVAH-ROHI**
  - "Jehovah my Shepherd"

When Elder Kendal came in, he said, *"Tonight, I am going to talk about the names of God."* Well, I was so glad because he was definitely one of the best teachers *(in my opinion)* who taught Bible Study. Whenever I leave from the study after he teaches, I have **no** questions to ask, as he quenches my thirst to learn about God and His Word.

CHAPTER FORTY-ONE
"I AM"—A POEM

One of the gifts God gave me was the ability to express my feelings through poetry. I want to share the following one with you because there is yet another name of God: **"I AM."**

Looking at a maze that was set before me, having been made up with many situations—fornication, lasciviousness, reveling, envying, and a beginning and an end—but between them are many pathways. For some to enter in, it may take a lifetime to find their way. Others may give up because of the many failed attempts. Some seem to make themselves comfortable where they are, unaware of the danger of staying.

The paths interconnect with one another, trying to keep you from leaving. There are many narrow hallways leading to many locked doors without keys. How many times will you knock on a door you cannot get in?

What drives you to pursue eternity? Why are you so persistent in finding your way? Is that which is at the end worth it? How do you even know that He is there?

Some have searched for a lifetime and never found their way. I won't stay locked in a maze, knowing that there's a beginning and an end. Faith will see me through the middle, and for those corridors and locked doors without keys, faith will get me through them.

Those who doubt that there is a beginning and an end, faith will show me. For those who went before me in the beginning but have not seen the end, faith will carry me over them. I came to a maze that was set before me. I entered it in faith, knowing the beginning and the end. It was that which was in between—the things I could not have seen because of the distance from "I AM"—although, in the corridors, His voice guided me through the labyrinth to the light.

Now that I am on the other side, I wish to go back, knowing what I've been through and trying to find my way to the light. Now that I have the light, it's too bright to keep inside when so many are on the other side still waiting. I—yes, I—could be a beacon unto them.

"And God said unto Moses, 'I AM THAT I AM.' And He said,
'Thus shalt thou say unto the children of Israel:
I AM hath sent me unto you.'"
~ Exodus 3:14 ~

CHAPTER FORTY-TWO
THE SCATTERED, LOST SHEEP

As I walked through the town and saw all of the people who are disconnected from God, it saddened me. So many people were walking around in circles their whole life—the same faces I saw every morning while on my way to school or on my way home from work. They're lost and didn't even know it. I saw them when they walked up and down the same streets, near a corner store, or close to a liquor store. It saddened me to see them use milk crates for sitting on, trying to appear comfortable where they were. They were alcoholics or drug addicts, lost in their addictions. No doubt, they felt abandoned or like they were the black sheep of their family.

How is it possible to get close to the lost without becoming lost yourself? It seems like we have to wait for them to come to meetings, like NA or AA. That's the place to share with them our strengths and hopes. What about those who are still sick and suffering out there on the corners? How do we reach them before death does? How can I explain to them that death is at their door when their door is wide open to death, and he gives them what they want; a false sense of comfort? How can I compete with that, Lord? How does one convince them that they have been scattered by the wolf for the slaughter?

Turned By Grace

God said to use a lost sheep — one that has been scattered like them and once walked with death. He needs them to see the sheep of His flock and how He looked after them, to keep at bay those who would cause them harm. What they need to see is newly-found sheep, being shepherded by Him.

"I am the Good Shepherd, but they do not recognize My voice. I call for them, but they do not answer; for they hear the voice of another, which frightens them. He uses fear to control them. Their flesh has been ripped from their bones, and their gashing lacerations are infested, yet they stay through the agony of it all.

"For such a time as this have I delivered you. I will place you around them, so they might see what I have done for you. All you need to do is follow after Me, and your walk will tell the story. You need not boast of what the Lord has done for you. Just let them see, for their eyes are hungry for another lifestyle.

"My son, you asked why I left you out there for so long. Here is your answer: Many are still suffering from addiction and have no clue why, but you have been shown what few believe exist. I have blessed you to do what many could not: You heard his voice and know that he is after generations of sons and daughters.

"So, here begins your journey from which your past has brought you to. You are more than ready for that which I prepared you for, and know that whom the Son has delivered and set free is free, indeed — for the victory has already been won. I just need the battle to exist. I can't have a victory without a battle. Now that I have laid out the light of your path, also know: To whom much is given, from him much will be required."

CHAPTER FORTY-THREE
THE NEW STUDENT

"These things have I spoken to you, that My joy might remain in you, and that your joy might be full."
~ John 15:11 ~

Almost two years had passed since I last indulged in using any form of mind-altering substance. I was still in school, focused on obtaining my GED. I switched to Union County College in Plainfield simply because I didn't want to wait for a bus in the cold. While in class, I made it a point to sit in front of the class to avoid distractions. One thing I recalled from the days of my youth was that those in the back of the class would fool around and not pay attention to the teacher. Strangely enough, even as adults, nothing had changed. Well, that's not entirely true. **I CHANGED.** I was always on time to class and submitted my work when it was due. I was making significant progress! Soon, I would feel confident enough to take the GED test.

One February day, a new student named Wanda came to class. She appeared very scared, so I spoke to her when she passed by my desk. That day, she sat two seats behind me. In noticing that she was Latino, I thought at first that she might have been in the wrong classroom because the one next door was all Latino pupils. After a couple of weeks went by, she was noticeably more comfortable and began to relax. Wanda and I would be in the same group sometimes, so we often discussed our assignments.

From time to time, I would glance over at Wanda while in class when she wasn't looking my way. She was very pretty, and I was especially fond of the way she spoke. She sounded so cute. I found out later she was from Puerto Rico. I wasn't looking for a girlfriend at the time, though. I was laser-beam focused on getting my GED, determined not to be sidetracked. Plus, I had been celibate for almost two years and simply wasn't looking to get involved in an intimate relationship with anyone. The women in my class didn't understand why I wasn't trying to flirt with any of them. I had my reasons…

I was still on my quest to learn who I was in God. **(Believe me when I say: *It is time-consuming but definitely worth it!*)** Before coming to know God for myself, I never thought I could have a relationship such as the one I had established with Him. After messing up my first chance at a peaceful and wholesome life, I had no plans whatsoever of bumbling my way through my second chance. To think: A lot of people never get a second try, so I intended to make the most of it.

I still worked for Deacon Jones at his restaurant in Plainfield. Sometimes, I did some overnight work for him at Newark's Penn Station, washing the tiles on the walls. What was most interesting to me about those visits was watching the people who were there at night. The first couple of times, Deacon Jones took me there to show me what he needed to be done. After that, I caught the train alone and, when I was done, rode it back home. Working with the Deacon kept me very busy on the weekends. There were some days we would finish a catering job on a Saturday, and he would drop me off at home at 3:00 in the morning—just to return at 5:30 so that we could start preparing at the restaurant across the street from the church. After I finished, I would then go to the service and then return to the restaurant to work my shift. Deacon would often ask me, *"Tell me what scripture Bishop spoke from today."* I think he was trying to make sure I was paying attention and stayed awake, especially after getting little to no sleep.

I liked being around Deacon Jones as I watched him go about handling different situations. He also asked me to help him with the New Beginnings meetings in Plainfield. One morning, around 2:00 a.m., we were on our way to New York to a fish market to purchase some fish for his restaurant. He would take me a lot of places with him, and we would talk and share a lot with each other. On this particular trip, I remember him telling me that he was going to preach God's Word, and I believed him.

I took a liking to Deacon Jones the first time I saw him at morning prayer at the transitional house. I recall that it was during the Thursday morning prayer that he held when I read from Psalms 41. I also clearly remember the day God told me He was going to put me under the Deacon's care; it was a couple of days before the 4th of July back in 2002. At the time, I was looking for some flyers in the Mercy House when God said to me, *"As soon as you get out of the program, you will begin working for Deacon Jones."* I was pleased. Deacon is a God-fearing man. Although he is only a couple of years older than me, he is my big brother in Christ. I enjoy being with him and am glad God placed me with him.

CHAPTER FORTY-FOUR
SUDDENLY, I CHANGED

Meanwhile, in school, some of the ladies were getting more and more curious about me. One even asked if I was gay. I laughed at first and then asked her, "Why would you ask me **that** question?"

"Because you keep to yourself and hardly ever talk to us," she said.

I explained to her that I was living a celibate lifestyle. "I know me," I continued. "If I start messing around, playing with y'all, it might lead me to do something I am not ready to do yet. To answer your question: No, I am not gay."

"So, you do like women?"

"Yes. I very much **LOVE** women, but I am not ready for a relationship. What made you ask me **THAT** question?"

She sat still for a moment before responding. "There are some women here who think you're handsome, but **YOU** act as if we're not even in the room with you."

I smiled at the compliment and said, "Oh, I see y'all. I just can't be distracted right now. My whole purpose in being here is to get my GED."

A day later, we were doing some geometry work on the blackboard. When it was Wanda's turn, she brushed my arm as she passed. She looked back at me and apologized. I smiled and said, *"That's okay."* While she was at the board solving her problem, I was watching her instead of looking at the problem being solved. As she returned to her seat, I found myself gawking at her.

I cannot explain what happened. I wish there were something I could tell you to justify the sudden change that came over me. What was worse was that I didn't want to consult with God to ask for help with the situation. I do acknowledge that I felt a familiar spirit. The issue I had was that I liked that feeling, even though it was contrary to what God was doing in my life. My flesh spoke to me loud and clear — and I heard every word. My flesh wanted Wanda, but I knew it would be wrong. Plus, relationships in my past hadn't gone too well for me. I would get what I wanted and soon after my fleshly needs were satisfied, I didn't want them anymore. Plainly put: It was just about the sex for me. I did **NOT** want to start doing that again.

So, even though I gawked at Wanda, I held back from trying to manipulate her for my own selfish needs.

It seemed as if the harder I tried **NOT** to act out in my flesh, the more my flesh desired her. That was precisely what I was trying to avoid! I was soon distracted from concentrating on my schoolwork, and the blouses Wanda would wear seemed to draw even more of my attention to her. In being honest, there were some days I would be in my seat and couldn't get up on account of my flesh processing lustful images of her. That, of course, made it impossible for me to concentrate in class. The battle between my spirit-man and flesh were betwixt.

The same day that Wanda touched me, while I was eating lunch in the cafeteria, a lady came over to my table and said, *"Hello."* I looked up and said, *"Hi."*

"My friend asked me to come over here to tell you that she likes you," she said.

"Who is your friend?"

She pointed and said, *"Her."*

When I followed the direction of her finger, I said to myself, *"Aww, man. This is **NOT** a good thing."* "Her" was Wanda. She smiled a seductive smile at me, then her friend walked away. I knew I was in trouble.

The weekend had come and gone, and Monday arrived. That day, I started to pay a little more attention to Wanda. I would glance at her from the corner of my eye because I didn't want her to know I was looking at her. I thought to myself, *"Maybe we could just be friends and help each other with schoolwork."*

By the beginning of March, Wanda and I would walk through the hallway talking and sitting together at lunch. We would search for places where we could be alone while at school, too. One day, I asked if I could see her after school, but she said, *"There's something I have to tell you before we go any further."* What she told me felt like an ice-cold bucket of water was poured over my head.

"I am a divorcee. My ex and I still live under the same roof."

After a moment of awkward silence, I said, *"Now you want to tell me this? Why would you even send your friend over to me to let me know you liked me when you still live in the house with your husband – or is he your ex-husband?"* It sounded like she was trying to run game on me because what she told me was something I would say when I used to mess with two and three women at a time. *"Look, I am not trying to break up anyone's family."*

"Jeff, I am not lying to you. He already has another woman. We haven't been together for years now."

"Right now, this is too much for me to digest. Let me think about this," I replied.

We returned to class, but what she told me kept me distracted for the rest of that day.

Once home, my flesh said, *"Who cares whether or not she's telling you the truth? You see how aroused she makes you. Just when you want to take her to a motel, she chooses to tell you about her "situation." Come on, man! What do you care? Are you going to marry her right now? What's the problem?"* My goodness. I was all up in my flesh! I wondered where God was when I needed him. Why was it that I only heard what my flesh wanted?

Jeffrey G. Mitchell, Sr.

I was in a hardcore battle with my flesh. I knew it was wrong to be with Wanda. She also had children from her marriage. Maybe if they got some type of counseling, they might be able to reconcile their union...

CHAPTER FORTY-FIVE
PREDATORIAL INSTINCTS

My God, my heart is crying out! My flesh is weak. I gave up my virtue too soon. The door to salaciousness caused the enemy to laugh at me. My thoughts are now consumed with desires of my flesh. I gave access to lasciviousness. What I see looks innocent through my eyes, but my flesh distorts the image in my mind so that it becomes a part of memories of my past — old memories that would entice me to do whatever my flesh wanted to do, all while my spirit wanted no part.

Wrestling for my soul, I profess that I am a new creature in Christ Jesus. How can this be what I desire? My fleshly desires are pulling at me from opposite ends. When I do something good that makes me feel connected to my spirit, it seems like I am on the path of righteousness.

A whirlwind of confusion comes upon me out of nowhere.

Glory to shame. Who's to blame? The deed was mine, but my mind led me down a road covered in shame. My soul cries out, *"My flesh is weak!"* Am I to blame, when I no longer am in control of my thoughts? My pain is deep; deeper than I can explain. My soul cries out for a change.

God, how long will You allow this pain to go on? No longer am I in control. Demons have gathered around my soul, taunting and manipulating me. How much longer must I put up with them?

"My son, the fortress is strong, and the foundation is deep — deeper than you know. I am bringing you to a place where the lusts of this world can no longer harm you. My Word have I hid in your heart. Deep within the scriptures, you are free. You will find peace from an enemy that put so many of My sons in the 'Hall of Shame.' Blessed is he who puts his trust in Me, for grace and mercy shall he see."

"And my temptation which was in my flesh, ye despised not, nor rejected; but received me as an angel of God, even as Christ Jesus."
~ Galatians 4:14 ~

How is it that I can be so intoxicant with the love of a woman, when You know, Lord, that she is not right for me. If I knew me like You know me, would that have made a difference in how I would choose a woman? Can it be that her beauty was so intoxicating, I see only what I wanted to see? I chose to not pay much attention to what she did or said because it irritated me, so I looked the other way for as long as I could. Intoxicated by her love, I wanted to be with her. With the lovely vision of her through my eyes, I did not want to see that she was not the one for me.

Tell me, God: Is this where I say, **"HELP!"** Because I am unable to see what You see for me, her beauty is a distraction. It covers what she does, not allowing me to see that we were not meant to be. I justified the things that irritated me because she would spend a night with me...another shot of her love intoxicated me. Now, I hope she can be whom You, Lord, would choose for me.

What will it take for me to see that choosing a woman seems to be something I can't seem to get right? Time after time, the choices I've made were from the lust of my flesh. I never take the time to see her as a friend or who she is by just talking with her. Why does my predatorial instinct take over me?

With honesty, I can say I need to change the way I look at women. If I want to find a woman who can make me say, *"I fell in love with you for who you are and not only what I see,"* is there still hope for me? Can I change my predator ways? Sometimes, I would speak and be the perfect gentleman. I would say all the right things, while staying away from words that would trigger my predatorial instincts and have me prowling, looking for a weakness or a sign that there lurks a lustful spirit on her.

Why does intimacy come before marriage in my life? Why can't I wait until I get married before having sex? Abba, I need to find a way to see Your beautiful daughters differently. My way is definitely not Your way.

"You are so caught up in what you see, son. It's distracting you from recognizing that it is a lure. Some things that are enticing are sometimes the opposite of what men want. What is behind that which you lust after?"

I hear you, God. I hear you…

CHAPTER FORTY-SIX
LUSTFUL SPIRITS

I was awakened to that lustful spirit in my life. For many years, I saw nothing wrong with the way I treated women. I used them to fulfill my fleshly needs and, once I was done with them, found a way to break free. I would explain to them that it was my fault and that they would be better off without me. How many abortions was I a part of? I was selfish and didn't want any woman to carry my seed until its birth. What I thought was typical was really the spirit of lust that manipulated me. I became a "Master Manipulator." I would say anything I could just to get what I wanted, only to realize time and again that my flesh would hunger again for someone new to conquer.

I was covered up, hidden in my addiction. I prowled, following the lust of my flesh, all while being manipulated myself by something unseen: the spirit of lust. No longer an addict, I was able to see that my drug addiction was likely covering up that lustful spirit.

Lust is a generational curse…I came to learn. I thought the curse was the drugs, but they served to camouflage the real perpetrator. Even as I became aware of its presence, I still permitted my flesh to have control over me. I indulged in something I knew I no longer wanted to do, but I couldn't stop.

I continued having relations with Wanda and, at times, would ask God, *"Why can't I stop doing what my flesh wants?"*

"O wretched man that I am!
Who will deliver me from this body of death?"
~ Romans 7:24 ~

My **heart** wanted more of God in my life, but my **flesh** sought out its own gratification—which kept me in constant warfare in my mind.

You see, I knew the spirit of addiction well. It was familiar to me. I could tell when it was trying to manipulate me to use drugs again. The spirit of lust, though? It's an old spirit that dwelled within me since my youth, except I never knew it was there.

Once aware of the spirit of lust's presence, I prayed to God for my deliverance. I asked Him, *"Why deliver me from drugs, only to let me find out about the spirit of lust that's on me?"* I had no control over the way my flesh reacted. I was in desperate need of God's delivering power. I no longer wanted to be manipulated by that spirit of lust, which was ever-present with me.

God, I seem to have a thorn that has made itself known to me—one that, under the cover of drugs, went unknown for many years. It tried to make me feel guilty about my relationship with You. My heart belongs to You, Abba, but I battle with my flesh to keep my mind from recalling thoughts from my past.

My flesh wants to draw me back into a worldly lifestyle, using the lust of my flesh. Since the spirit of addiction has no more influence over me, lust is using my desire to be with a woman and attempting to put distance between us, God. Do You suppose my testimony could be a threat to the enemy?

Why have You bestowed Your grace on me, when I have done nothing to deserve Your mercy, God? Who am I that You would set Your eyes on me and transform my heart from the darkness this world has taught me?

Through the love of Christ, my heart has been touched in a way the world could never darken again. I come before You, Lord, as a servant, knowing that I serve the Most High King of kings and Lord of lords, to whom all power has been given. With You, all things are possible. I will not stop seeking You because of my flesh, for I know that in You is the power to deliver me from all evil. The will is present for me to do good, but doing what is good doesn't always happen for me. Father, my deeds are before You. Cover me with Your grace until the righteousness of the Lord sees me through.

"For I am persuaded that neither death nor life, nor angel nor principalities nor powers, nor things present nor things to come, nor height nor depth, nor any other created thing, shall be able to separate us from the love of God, which is in Christ Jesus our Lord."
~ **Romans 8:38-39** ~

CHAPTER FORTY-SEVEN
SIN'S TRIP TO DALLAS

At the school, they hosted a job fair, so I filled out some applications. On May 17, 2004, I started a job at UPS. I was looking for medical benefits, which was the primary reason I took the job. The hours were from 3:30 a.m. to 9:00 a.m. The only downside to those hours was that I had to catch the last bus—the 114 to Bridgewater—which came around 12:40 a.m. to Plainfield, leaving me with about a two-hour wait until my shift started.

I was a pre-loader. The other workers and I would load the trucks with the packages for the drivers' deliveries. I was assigned three trucks to load. The packages would come down a conveyor line onto a belt that was in front of me. The trucks were parked behind. The good thing was that I learned fast. The three trucks I loaded were all heading to Plainfield, so I was familiar with some of the streets that were listed on the load charts. Within a couple of months, I was loading so fast, my supervisor would ask me to help other people on the line with loading their trucks!

When my shift ended, I would then go home, take a quick shower, and go to school. By this time, Wanda had already tested for and received her GED and started working. I continued to make progress in class, but I would often get tired in computer class from staring at the screen. Now and then, I would get up to take a walk in the school's courtyard to grab a breath of fresh air and to give my eyes a welcomed break.

By November, I was only working on the weekends at the restaurant because I wanted to spend more time working towards my GED. Once I obtained it, I could then begin courses to become a Counselor. I wanted to be a counselor to give back and help others who battled with addictions.

Wanda's job sent her to Denver for on-the-job training *(her position required she be trained in different states)*. She called me one day and asked me to visit her that weekend. I said yes, and she made all of the travel arrangements for me.

It was the weekend before Thanksgiving. I thought to myself, *"Should I bring my Bible with me? Do I want to visit a church while I am there?"* The Spirit told me, **"You need to take your Bible with you."** Plus, I had never flown on a plane before, so I could read to take my mind off of the flight, although it was likely they would show a movie while in flight.

As I stood in line waiting to get my ticket that Wanda had already paid for, I started thinking about whose church I could visit while I was there. When it was my turn, I told the attendant my name and destination. She said, *"I have a ticket for you, but it's not to Denver. This ticket is for Dallas."* Hmm… Maybe the job moved her again. I accepted the ticket and headed to the gate to wait for boarding.

I remember asking Wanda to make sure I had a window seat. As I boarded and found my seat, I was thinking about Dallas and how I didn't know any preachers there. God then said, *"You are going to see Bishop T.D. Jakes."* I was **overjoyed! God surprised me with the trip!** He knew in my heart I wanted to see Bishop Jakes for myself, ever since I heard that one year, the men in the transitional house went to see Bishop Jakes. In 2002, I asked God to find a way for me to go as well.

The plane began its taxi down the runway. I was filled with joy behind how God remembered what I had asked of Him. I wasn't even nervous about my first time on a plane, although my ears clogged up as we started the ascent into the sky. I watched as the ground got farther away, and then I was looking down at the clouds as we flew over them. Once we leveled off, I started to relax. While looking at the view out the window, I thought about how beautiful and peaceful it was up there.

When we arrived in Dallas, the sun was setting, leaving behind an impressive view of the sky. I truly enjoyed the flight. Once we departed off of the plane, Wanda was waiting for me. We grabbed my luggage and headed to the hotel. As soon as we got there, I went to the front desk and asked how far we were from Bishop Jake's church, The Potter's House. I was told only 30 minutes.

Once in the room, I told Wanda I wanted to go to church on Sunday, as there was a preacher I wanted to see while I was in Dallas. She said, *"Okay. We can go."* We then hugged, kissed, and said how much we missed each other. We got comfortable, cuddled up on the bed, and kissed some more. In my lust, I uttered words to capture the intensity of the moment—the same ones I used when talking to God; however, the *intent* of my words changed. When I spoke them to Wanda, they were from the lust of my flesh…a part of me that had yet to fully surrender to God.

The experience was very confusing. I knew that God brought me to Dallas to see Bishop Jakes. He had to know that my flesh was going to want Wanda as soon as we were alone together.

> *"When thou sittest to eat with a ruler, consider diligently what is before thee. Be not desirous of his dainties: for they are deceitful meat. How was I to know that I would have to choose whose table I will find my delight? For the ruler of this world's existence is not seen, but has the capability and the means to influence my mind with whispers of my childhood."*
> ~ **Proverbs 23:1-3** ~

As my heart darkened, the enemy prepared a place for me at his table. Knowing my likes and dislikes gave him an advantage over me. How do I battle that which is not seen? Even when I sit at his table, I eat alone. He has nothing new to offer me, besides my childhood appetite. Although he had generations to perfect his plan against me, sooner or later I will have my fill at your table, for my heart has already been changed. How long do you think you can keep feeding my childhood appetite? As my heart changes, my desire will, too.

After Wanda and I were intimate, I would always find myself taking a shower and asking God for forgiveness for both

Wanda and me. I knew not when God was going to deliver me from the lustful spirit. I did, however, know that since He delivered me from drugs, He would deliver me from that, too.

In the early morning, I laid on my face in prayer and worship, professing that I was **MORE** than a conqueror in Christ. I vowed to continue giving God the glory, despite my situation. *"God, You know my heart and how much I want to serve You in spirit and in truth, for in Your righteousness, I am delivered. Your Word says in Proverbs 23:7, 'For as he thinks in his heart, so is he.' Lord, my heart is set on You, and my desires are those which You called me for."*

CHAPTER FORTY-EIGHT
DESTINY'S HIDDEN HISTORY

On Sunday, November 21, 2004, Wanda and I were seated in The Potter's House close to the altar. Even better than that, Bishop Jakes was there to bring forth the Word of God. I was happy because he could have been out visiting another church. He is well-known and a great man of God. I was so very happy for the opportunity to be in his presence.

The Word of God that day came from the Book of 1st Samuel 17:38-39. Bishop Jakes' topic was, "This is no time to change." Following are the notes I took while he preached:

I have to serve the Lord. I was called according to His purpose. Something about my destiny is hidden in my history. The gifts God gave me are for my divine purpose. Be consistent in what I do, and it will bring forth great results. Do not quit. Focus on what God has spoken and where He has placed me. Be faithful unto Him, the One who brought me out of the land of bondage. Everything that I was going through was for this era in my life. Small things are important to great people. The level of my opposition tells me about the level of my destiny. The battles I overcome in my private life will catapult me in life. Get ready! God is about to take me to another level.

After the Word was preached, people approached the altar to accept Christ as their Savior. I looked at Wanda and asked, *"Are you saved?"* She said she was. When a man passed by me, I felt in my spirit God telling me that when he comes back to give him a copy of my poem, "A New Son of Mine."

When service was over and we were on our way back to the hotel, we stopped to grab a bite to eat. *"What did you think about the service, Wanda?"*

"I enjoyed it. I would like to go to a church like that back home."

"You should come to church with me one Sunday," I offered.

"Why did you want to go to The Potter's House, Jeff?"

I explained to her about me being in the program and hearing about how the men attended a service there one year. I went on to tell her how in 2002, I asked God to make a way for me someday, as it was something in my heart that I wanted God to do for me.

She then asked me, *"Do you think God put us together for a reason?"*

"I am not sure," I said with all honesty. *"What we are doing is a sin, and God is without sin. There is no sin in the One who died for sin. I am puzzled about us. I love you, but I am in sin being with you. Still, God allowed me to come out here to visit The Potter's House to see Bishop Jakes. I know there is something I am supposed to do for God. I feel strongly about letting people know there is life after*

addiction and deliverance in Christ Jesus for any situation. Sin in our lives has separated us from the love of God."

I believe that the spirit of lust that I battle with is my opposition. It, of course, doesn't want me to follow after the things of God. The lustful spirit would rather I continue in my lust of the flesh and get the gratification from it.

Ohhhh, but there is a Comforter who dwells in me to do well and follow after what **GOD** has for me!

Once back in the hotel room, I packed my things, preparing to head back home. I felt a sadness come over me because I had to leave. Although I enjoyed my time spent with Wanda, I also felt an overwhelming appreciation for God. On our trip to the airport, we both expressed how we wished we had more time to spend together, but I had to leave because I had to return to work the next day.

During the return flight, I thought about the message Bishop Jakes preached. I asked God, *"What do You mean that 'my destiny was hidden in my history'?"*

The answer was instantaneous and thorough: *"That which held you in bondage was that which brought you to Me. Remember how misplaced you were? You may have been alive, but there was no life in you. Death was knocking at your door, wanting to relieve the pain you were in. Remember how you cried tears of pain, asking Me to help bring you out of that which you yourself could not do? Remember when you started to hear the voice of the enemy and the way he tried to manipulate you, saying that you were like a god — able to keep getting high while others in your family had stopped?*

Turned By Grace

Addiction and bondage were how the enemy manipulated you. The fear of the unknown fueled your addiction, while bondage kept you from your destiny. The enemy masked generational curses through your addictions. So, if the chains of addiction were never broken, he would then rely on the bitterness, envy, and strife in your heart."

CHAPTER FORTY-NINE
11 SCRIPTURES FOR FOCUSING AND CLEANSING

God said to me: *"Therefore, I have placed in you My words, which you will need to combat against a hardened heart. Focus on My words and cleanse your heart."*

I share with you the following passages of scripture that helped me both focus and cleanse:

- "Jesus answered and said unto him, 'Verily, verily, I say unto thee: Except a man be born again, he cannot see the Kingdom of God.'" ~ John 3:3 ~
- "Therefore, if any man be in Christ, he is a new creature: old things are passed away; behold, all things are become new." ~ 2nd Corinthians 5:17 ~
- "But seek ye first the Kingdom of God and His righteousness; and all these things shall be added unto you." ~ Matthew 6:33 ~
- "Draw nigh to God, and He will draw nigh to you. Cleanse your hands, ye sinners; and purify your hearts, ye double-minded." ~ James 4:8 ~
- "He that dwelleth in the secret place of the Most High shall abide under the shadow of the Almighty." ~ Psalms 91:1 ~

- "Now, faith is the substance of things hoped for, the evidence of things not seen." ~ Hebrews 11:1 ~
- "And I will raise Me up a faithful priest that shall do according to that which is in Mine heart and in My mind: and I will build him a sure house; and he shall walk before Mine anointed forever." ~ 1st Samuel 2:35 ~
- "The hand of the LORD was upon me, and carried me out in the Spirit of the LORD, and set me down in the midst of the valley which was full of bones." ~ Ezekiel 37:1 ~
- "Thy Word is a lamp unto my feet, and a light unto my path." ~ Psalms 119:105 ~
- "My son, give Me thine heart and let thine eye observe My ways." ~ Proverbs 23:26 ~
- "These things I have spoken to you, that My joy may remain in you, and that your joy may be full." ~ John 15:11 ~

God then said, *"For My words will keep you, and My grace will sustain you through your walk with Me. The enemy will be persistent in making you feel that you are not worthy of My love and try to make you feel guilty about your sin. Speak My words over your life, My son. Hide them in your heart."*

CHAPTER FIFTY
PROFICIENCY IS KEY

During my cab ride home from the airport, I knew I had to go to work, but I was so tired. When I finally made it, I quickly laid my suitcase on the floor and changed into my work clothes. I had just enough time to walk and catch the last bus. As I made my way to the bus stop, I thought about how awesome God is. I had gone all the way to Dallas, seen Bishop Jakes at The Potter's House, and still made it back to work on time. I may have been tired, but I sang praises to God all the way to the bus stop!

Then, all 11 of the scriptures shared in the previous chapter starting coming forth from me. I kept saying them over and over as I continued walking. Even on the bus, I said them to myself under my breath. God's hand was on me and, for some reason, He kept on blessing me — even when I felt I was unworthy of His goodness.

As I sat upstairs in the break area waiting for my shift to start, I looked through my Bible, trying to understand why God gave me those specific passages. It seemed as if they were to encourage me in my walk with God. When I reach each of them, they appeared to be a set of instructions for me.

Turned By Grace

Roughly 15 minutes before the start of my shift, I usually headed down to set up my packages for the trucks. Some of the trucks would return with packages that weren't delivered, so I liked to place them back on the shelf where they belonged. The Piscataway facility where I worked had eight lines that carried packages that were presorted by the unload department for the loaders. The job was relatively easy, especially once I learned the load methods. Doing three trucks at a time became a breeze!

Six months into the job, I could load all three of my trucks quickly without leaving piles of packages around my area. I noticed some others would not have been able to say the same. I would think to myself, *"Why do they have so many packages outside of their trucks?"* One good thing about being done early with my loading was that my supervisor would often ask me to help out other loaders on the line. I didn't mind because that meant I would get some extra hours in my paycheck.

At the end of my shift that day, all I wanted was my bed. Thankfully, the school was closed until after the Thanksgiving holiday. I only had two more days to work at UPS because they had given us off for the holiday. **Ahhh! Four days off.** I planned on catching up on my rest.

CHAPTER FIFTY-ONE
GOD'S INSPIRATION IN POEM

Today, I have a lot to be thankful for. I am grateful for how God turned my life around in just a couple of years. I never knew life could be so good after being an addict. He keeps me working, too. There have been times I've had two jobs while taking classes to get my GED. I love the fact that I am learning how to live a Christian lifestyle through Bible study and a relationship with God.

Most of all, I am grateful for my relationship with God and every new day He gives me. I know it was nothing I've done to deserve His mercy. I think back on all the times I asked for God's help while sitting in a tub of cold bath water, trying to slow down the pounding of my heart, not knowing if I would breathe my last breath after my heart would burst. As I sat in the tub, I would grab my wallet from my pants from off the floor to look at the pictures of my children. If I were to die at that moment, I wanted my children to be the very last thing seen by me.

Very bleak, right?

Lord, it was your mercy that saved me from the depths of my hell. I was caught up in the lust of my flesh. Your mercy didn't care that I was a sinner, held in bondage with no hope.

Turned By Grace

For this cause, have I cried out for a Savior; one who would not judge me while helping me…one who would not condemn me for the sins of my past. Lord, I was in need of help, and You sent Your Son long before I was born to be my Savior.

As I pondered about God's goodness, I thought about the poem "BLESS" and how He delivered me from the hand of my enemy. Today, I share "BLESS" in my travels. If, for some reason, I may not have given it to a person it was intended for, I say to God, *"If You want them to have Your poem, bring them again in my travels, and I will hand them Your poem."*

Because I was handing out His poem "BLESS," God began to bless me with **more** poems. One of them He wrote through my spirit while I sat at the dining room table. It's called "My Beautiful Daughters." I remember the moment well. I had just finished writing a *different* poem when I looked up and saw my daughter in the kitchen washing a dish. I asked of God, *"Please write a poem for Your daughters."*

"Many daughters have done virtuously, but thou excellest them all. Favor is deceitful, and beauty is vain; but a woman that feared the LORD, she shall be praised."
~ Proverbs 31:29-30 ~

CHAPTER FIFTY-TWO
"MY BEAUTIFUL DAUGHTERS"
A POEM

Independent though you may think, yet you may never be complete without having a relationship with Me. Daughters, I can show you how beautiful I made you. From Me you came, so come back to Me, and I will show you the dreams I dreamt and the beauty I placed within that can never be reached without having a relationship with Me.

First, I must cleanse the enemy from within; the hurt and pain that you carried from people and men who used you, while the emptiness of your heart confused you; while searching for a love that could never love you, only because you never looked towards the One who created you.

I will satisfy your every need spiritually and teach you how to be whom I created you to be. I won't confuse or mistreat you. I won't play those silly games, misleading you. But I will challenge you to respect yourself as a daughter of Mine. I will show you why I called you if you reconnect with Me, instead of connecting with men who only want to show you their physical love.

I will raise a prince for My queen. If you choose to connect with Me, no more foolishness will there be. Set your eyes on Me and watch all the dreams I spoke to you come true because you chose a relationship with Me.

~~~~~~~~~~

As I would share this poem to let women know they are God's Beautiful Daughters, I once saw a nice young lady on the bus I ride home from UPS. Although I didn't have any of my poems with me at the time, I thought about giving her a copy of "My Beautiful Daughters." I then asked myself, *"Are you giving her the poem because you want to meet her or is it to bring her into a relationship with God?"* You see, even when I have good intentions to do the right thing, I have to stop and look at what motives are in play.

Am I doing it in the Spirit of God or am I using His poem for my own fleshly needs?

I want to be used by God to help people find their way to Him, but sometimes, my flesh gets in the way and wants to manipulate the situation.

CHAPTER FIFTY-THREE
STRENGTH IN DELIVERANCE

Meanwhile, at UPS, peak season had arrived. The number of packages was almost double the normal amount. We handled an estimated 50,000 packages in a four-hour shift during the regular season, but because of the upcoming Christmas holiday, it was not uncommon to handle well over 100,000 packages on some nights. Because of the increased workload, they had us working eight-hour shifts. The extra money was truly a blessing. The way I heard people talking about how difficult the month of December was, I expected things to be more of a challenge for me. It wasn't. I continued to do my job with ease.

As I was preparing to leave one Friday after work, my supervisor walked over to me and said, *"I've been watching you. I like the way you do your job here."* What he asked me next showed God's favor on my life. **"Would you like to be a part-time supervisor at UPS?"**

"Can I give you my answer on Monday when I return?" I asked.

He nodded in agreement and said, "Okay. I want you to think about the offer. I believe you will make a good supervisor." I thanked him for even considering me.

I knew the company wanting me as a supervisor was nothing **BUT GOD**. *Wow!* I had only been with the company for seven months! That said a lot about how God was moving in my life. He was definitely preparing me for His glory.

As I thought it all through, I found it was an opportunity to learn some leadership skills in a supervisory position. Well, not to make **YOU**, Dear Reader, wait until Monday:

I ACCEPTED THE POSITION!

I officially began in January after our New Year's break. In 2005—**after working at UPS for only seven months and having three years of clean time**—I became a part-time supervisor!

That year, I began to truly feel the strength in my deliverance from heroin. It seemed, however, that every year, a test would come my way. In 2004, I saw a bundle of heroin on my way to school one day. I knew that if I had stopped to pick it up, I would be back in the pits of Hell. I had no desire to get burned.

Another time, I went on a party boat to go fishing with some friends. The person I was riding in the car with knew I was in recovery. Not only did he **KNOW**, but he also attended a New Beginnings meeting, too. I remember him because I was the one running it that night. While he and I were riding along 287 South, he lit up a joint and said, *"Sorry, Jeff, but I'm going to smoke this."* I **could have** said to him, *"Pull over and let me out,"* and then walk home…*but I didn't.*

Jeffrey G. Mitchell, Sr.

I prayed to God instead. *"God, please don't let me get a buzz or even smell that thing he is smoking."* I turned my head toward the window, let it down, and kept praying. *"Lord, let not the enemy have any victory over my life."* I even prayed against that spirit of addiction on the man who was smoking the joint. I then stopped and thought: *"If someone in another vehicle passes us by and happens to see him smoking a joint, they will surely think I'm getting high right along with him. Man, I got myself into some kind of situation here!"*

Later on, while on the party boat, I saw a lot of people who were drinking beer. Others even had boxes of wine they brought to drink. But me? I wanted to fish and relax. I looked around, trying to find someone else who wasn't drinking. I found no one. It seemed as if everyone on the boat was enjoying themselves by drinking alcohol. That made me look at myself and wonder about why I didn't care to do the things I used to do. Heck, less than five years prior, I would have brought along my own stuff and partied right alongside everyone else. That didn't stop me from enjoying myself, knowing that I didn't have to drink anymore to have fun.

CHAPTER FIFTY-FOUR
THE NEWNESS OF LIFE

My God, this journey I am on with You has me seeing the enemy at every turn in my life. The closer I get to You, the more inferior the enemy makes me feel. He tries to tell me I am unworthy of knowing You or being loved by You. For some reason, I have endured all that the enemy has put me through. The compulsion to revolve from my past lifestyle keeps me in humility and endlessly asking for guidance from You.

I am compelled to walk in this newness of life, for I know how dark my mind truly is and how much darker it wants to become. My thoughts are of evil, always with me. I am trying to understand the light I have been given to do well and to show a change in my lifestyle while I walk in the Spirit of God, but my flesh is contrary to my walk with You.

I used to live a worldly lifestyle and did that which was under the law, as well as what was against the law. I was subjected to man's judgment both in and out of the courts, for man will judge you for your deeds, whether they are the deeds of a good man or an evil man.

My distress comes from the evil thoughts that try to consume my mind, for which only I can judge. I know not to act on them, but that does not stop my mind and thoughts from conjuring up worldly images.

> *"And do not be conformed to this world; but be transformed by the renewing of your mind, that you may prove what is that good and acceptable and perfect will of God."*
> **~ Romans 12:2 ~**

CHAPTER FIFTY-FIVE
MY CONFESSION

Abba, remember when You said that You allowed me to stay in my addiction because I was carrying the weight and pain for others? Well, You must have known that leaving me in the deepness of the valley with all of those dry bones would cause me to have more than my share of character defects by the time You brought me out. I had conversations with the enemy in the deepness of the valley; talks of death and how he thought that at the age of 40, I had lived long enough.

I just want You to know what happened because my mind is always pondering and imagining on things of my past. I no longer want to remember and rarely do. I now want to reciprocate the love You've given unto me, but my thoughts are twisted and can be perverted, to the point where I am concerned about not being able to do that which I was called to do for You.

My comfort zone is under attack, aware of my situation. Change is inevitable if I want to have a future with You. Lead me, Abba, that my mind may be healed and transformed by the power of Christ as I journey with You — all while dealing with the lustfulness of my flesh and the images he wants me to dwell on.

As I lie in my bed struggling in my flesh with my past thoughts, there's frustration within me because of what I have done. My past and subconscious thoughts are wrestling against the newness of my heart because of that which I used to do but now no longer want or have any desire to do. My body wants to act on the desires of my flesh, while my heart desires to act spiritually.

There's a part of me that still likes what my flesh wants, but another part knows that it would be wrong. If I wasn't confused before, I am now, Lord. I am being pulled inward and outward, and it's frustrating me.

Why am I betwixt? I feel like a trio in one body. I know what's going on, but sometimes I feel like a spectator observing the goings-on between them. One of them wants to give me eternal life; the other is trying to make sure I am damned for eternity. How is it that the choice before me is not difficult to see, but doing what is right isn't always in me?

My God, why have You called me? I have so much pain in my heart, layers on top of pain that covers the hurt. This was Your choice for me? Years of pain I endured with a heart because I knew not how to express what it felt.

"Find out who you are, son. I see a treasure from where I am looking. Deep inside is an accumulation of wealth which I have stored in you. It's precious and valuable, but few tools of this world can reach it or get you near to it.

"Deep inside is where I placed it. Deep calling unto deep is where you have to go to get it. That sin which covers your heart is for

the closeness that keeps you close to Me so that you can seek Me to find the treasure I placed in you.

"I am a Father to many, but so few of My sons let me close enough to show them how precious I made them and the reason for their life. If only they knew how to look towards Me to find out who they are in Me. I want you to have the treasure I gave you and show you how truly blessed you could be. Instead, you look elsewhere for your treasure."

Abba, lead me back to You. Show me in Your Word how to get my heart in line with Yours, that I may do that which is in Your heart. Pray for me. Let the manifestation of Your Word come forth in my life. Position Your servant in the will of God that I may serve You in the calling I was called for. Rebuke the curse of lust off of my life, and let me walk in the Earth as a blessed man of God.

I know that the enemy places stumbling blocks on the paths of the righteous to delay or frustrate those who are the called of God. I know it's the love I feel today in my heart that keeps me pressing towards the dreams and revelation God has given me to stay the course with Him, no matter what stumbling blocks the enemy lays before me. The very Word of God will lift me in the Spirit right over them.

CONCLUSION

I was delivered from my addiction and came to know the power of deliverance from God as I matured as a Christian. He then started to reveal glimpses and pieces of my future to me.

After being out of school for 25 years, I finally earned my GED. God showed me sitting with young men, trying to help them find their way back in life.

I continue to battle with the lust of my flesh, even after countless times of going to the altar and being on my face at home, asking for deliverance. My cries for help have made me weary in my walk, for I see no end to the enemy's torment.

Although I continue to awake every morning believing that this is the day I will have victory over my enemy, **hope** is what I live for. **Purpose** is what drives me. Today, I have a purpose in my life once again, and I refuse to lie down and die, all because I may lose a battle here and there to my flesh.

See, I may not be able to say I am a "perfect Christian," but I am a Christian who is still fighting to see the glory of God in my life. Perhaps someday, **I will** be victorious over my flesh. I do know that I love God today with all of my heart, and if He isn't going to give up on me, then neither will I give up on me. ***By faith, this battle is won!***

"By faith, the walls of Jericho fell down after they were encircled for seven days."

~ **Hebrews 11:30** ~

Jeffrey G. Mitchell, Sr.

EVOLVING – A POEM

There's a lion that dwells within, but I see through the eyes of a lamb, while my heart beats of a young lion who wants to be free to explore and vocalize his roar. The lion is wild and has the instinct to hunt, so I feel his frustration as he lurks at what I see. Through the eyes of the lamb, I want to live a life of gentleness and peace, able to folly and play, but my posture is of a young lion waiting to swoop suddenly on his next prey.

So, I struggle with that which I see as a lamb and that which I do as a young lion. Their characteristics are as opposite as they are, but yet they dwell within looking at what I see. Hasty decisions and rage allow the lion to respond, scheming and planning while patrolling back and forth.

My heart beats of a young lion. My stomach is full of the flesh upon which I prey. My claws and teeth drip their blood, and my tongue laps it up, while my eyes roll back with pleasure. I am a predator.

See now my DNA, exposing a creature of habit…a predator lurking and observing while roaming free, helpless to change its destiny. How can you expect conversion when you've placed me in the jungle with instincts to hunt?

Turned By Grace

I see through the eyes of a lamb. The closest I came was when I was a whelp. Maybe then I had a chance to live as a lamb, but you waited until I developed as a young lion. For I am betwixt that which I desire and that which gratifies my flesh, as I struggle between life and death, seeing my past forever prowling over my shoulders, while viewing life in a blistering African heatwave, trying to find hope before hopeless stains my insight.

My heart feels the pain that my flesh desires. I truly try not to indulge the actions of my flesh, which causes remorse and shame to come upon me. My appearance is of a young lion; my destiny is to be a King, but my eyes see as a lamb who takes no pleasure through the actions of my flesh.

Jeffrey G. Mitchell, Sr.

ABOUT THE AUTHOR

Jeffrey G. Mitchell, Sr. was born in 1961 to James and Sheila Mitchell. He was the third of six children. Throughout the years, he has made many special memories with his older brother and sister that warm his heart to this day.

By the time Jeffrey became a teenager, he had indulged in smoking marijuana and drinking alcohol. Unknowingly, they became his enemy later in life. While in high school, he admittedly spent more time selling and using marijuana than going to class to earn his High School Diploma. He states, "The sad thing about that is I didn't even know where the library was in the school." That is significant because, in both elementary and junior high, he loved going to the library to read.

By the 1980s, Jeffrey was a high school dropout. That facet of his life led him to work countless jobs that led nowhere.

In the year 2000, Jeffrey's struggle with addiction to heroin had been ongoing for over ten years, all while attempting to get clean and be free from the spirit of addiction by visiting inpatient and outpatient clinics. His life quickly spun out of control. That same year, he was arrested and was given a choice: find a program and get clean OR spend three years behind bars. For him, that was a no-brainer. In 2001, he found and entered a Christian rehabilitation program.

At the age of 40, the enemy tried to convince Jeffrey that his life was over and that it was alright for him to die. When death came to his front door, it didn't even bother to knock.

BUT GOD! God's hand remained on Jeffrey the entire time he was in his addiction.

Today, he shares his testimony of strength against all the odds with others who are in addiction and believe there is no hope or future outside of the suffering.

Jeffrey G. Mitchell, Sr.

www.ingramcontent.com/pod-product-compliance
Lightning Source LLC
Chambersburg PA
CBHW071913110526
44591CB00011B/1664